AF658832

WOMEN IN MEGHALAYA

Women in Meghalaya

Soumen Sen

2026
Daya Publishing House®
A Division of
Astral International Pvt. Ltd.
New Delhi – 110 002

© *EDITOR*

First Published, 1992

Reprinted, 2026

ISBN: 978-81-7035-108-5 (Hardback)

Publisher's Note:

Every possible effort has been made to ensure that the information contained in this book is accurate at the time of going to press, and the publisher and author cannot accept responsibility for any errors or omissions, however caused. No responsibility for loss or damage occasioned to any person acting, or refraining from action, as a result of the material in this publication can be accepted by the editor, the publisher or the author. The Publisher is not associated with any product or vendor mentioned in the book. The contents of this work are intended to further general scientific research, understanding and discussion only. Readers should consult with a specialist where appropriate.

Every effort has been made to trace the owners of copyright material used in this book, if any. The author and the publisher will be grateful for any omission brought to their notice for acknowledgement in the future editions of the book.

All Rights reserved under International Copyright Conventions. No part of this publication may be reproduced, stored in a retrieval system, or transmitted in any form or by any means, electronic, mechanical, photocopying, recording or otherwise without the prior written consent of the publisher and the copyright owner.

Published by : **Daya Publishing House®**
A Division of
Astral International Pvt. Ltd.
– ISO 9001:2015 Certified Company –
4736/23, Ansari Road, Darya Ganj
New Delhi-110 002
Ph. 011-43549197
E-mail: info@astralint.com
Website: www.astralint.com

Printed at : **Replika Press Pvt. Ltd.**

Contents

1

INTRODUCTION

Soumen Sen

Social progress is closely linked with the role women play in society. It would be impossible to discuss the past, the present and the future of humanity without dwelling on the position of women. It must be admitted that women play a far greater role in society than we are aware of. It must also be admitted that for centuries they were denied their legitimate rights and position in society. They have not been assigned position commensurate to their role. One of the most glaring inconsistencies of historical societies is the inequality women suffer from. They have been relegated to a position subordinate or inferior to men. This is a legacy of several epochs. Man has assumed control of the productive means, shifting the woman to house work. She has been pushed to the background.

Growing awareness of this situation and of the need for improving the condition of women prompted the United Nations to declare 1975 as *International Women's Year* and the Years 1975-85 as the *UN Decade for Women: Equality, Development and Peace.* This decision testifies to the general recognition of the principle of equality of men and women and of the multidimensional roles women play in the society.

Under the auspices of the United Nations and national

governments, Women Studies began in a big way during the decade 1975-85. Although the decade ended in 1985, studies were not discontinued for the very simple reason that problems still persist and more data need to be generated for development policies and programmes. There is still need for interdisciplinary empirical studies on women to generate such data.

The academic community in particular has a responsibility in this regard. Empirical studies, before evolving plans for solving women's problems, can contribute in investigating the causes of gender disparity within the broader framework of social inequality.

In Indian context this becomes all the more important. Although women, especially the metropolitan women, have risen to higher levels in India and other South Asian countries, much have remained to be done to break the ageold prejudices determined by social and religious traditions. The inequality of women also stems from mass poverty and general backwardness. Modernisation in Indian context is, therefore, more of an artificial graft on the traditional and underdeveloped economy and society. The traditional role assigned to women in this society has restricted their mobility. In Hindu tradition, though women have been considered to be the prime source of strength as testified in the mythology and oral history and that theoretically they have a place of honour in the society, in practice lot of prejudices stand in the way of treating them as equal with men. Likewise, the Islamic tradition, though speaks of the principle of respect for women and that the Prophet declared, 'Paradise is at the foot of the mother', in reality the Muslim women are generally backward with neither respect nor any grace.

These prejudices, which often come in the way of the development of women, are to be broken to uplift the basic standards and help them cultivate their faculties for a fuller expression of their personalities. This means transcending the old polarized roles of female and masculine work and demands a new round of consciousness raising.

Is the situation different in the tribal settings of north-eastern region of India ? To an extent, yes. The prejudices that are noticed in the pan-Indian scenario are relatively absent here. With their household economic system, practice of shifting cultivation, the land holding pattern and egalitarian ethos, the society does not suffer from any prejudice against women. Particularly in Meghalaya, inhabited by the Khasi-Jaintias and the Garos, the matrilineal system protects, to a large extent, the position of women in the society. It will, therefore, be unfair to apply a single rigid definition of status in this societal context. At the same time a question may be raised whether matriliny has assigned a greater role to women. If so, what is the 'actual' in tradition ? It is also to be examined whether the responsibilities shouldered by women in the matrilineal system without access to power do not compromise their role and status in the social order. This question arises because women have no decision making authority, neither in the household nor in the socio-political power structure. Above all, the modes through which this tribal society has established linkages with wider social, cultural and economic system over the years need to be studied with appropriate parameters to understand the shift, if any, from traditional to modern. What is then, the 'actual' in the emerging (or already emerged) situation ? The basic issue is, therefore, to separate the myth from the reality.

To understand these processes and their implications, the Centre for Literary and Cultural Studies, North-Eastern Hill University, organised a Seminar on the *Status of Women in the Tribal Culture of Meghalaya,* in July 1988. The Seminar was sponsored by the North-Eastern Regional Centre of Indian Council of Social Science Research.

II

This collection contains the papers presented to the Seminar. The papers provide informations regarding traditional status and role of women in both the Khasi-Jaintia and Garo Societies and place these informations in a temporal framework to understand the processes of change.

Juanita War, dealing with the status of women in traditional Khasi culture, begins with a study of contrasts. Whereas in some societies the contributions of women are not fully acknowledged and indignity is inflicted on them, women in Khasi society enjoy a position of respect and grace. The brutal domination of one sex by another, as reflected in such practices as bride/wife burning, *devdasi*, *sati*, female foeticide, and aberrations like sexual assaults, are never to be seen in this society. The social and family organisations are such that there is greater freedom for women and both sexes contribute maximally for a cohesive social life. Customary laws have defined the roles assigned to men and women. In the traditional Khasi society men are the warriors and protectors, tillers, hunters, administrators, priests etc. Their roles and duties are in domains outside the house. This is symbolised by the bow and arrow placed on a white cloth at the naming ceremony of a baby boy. Women have the roles of mothers, housekeepers, custodians of family property, helpers in the fields and groves. At the naming ceremony of a baby girl, the symbols for the roles she will play are *ka khoh* (sling basket) and *u star* (rope to carry the basket). The uniqueness of the role and status of women can be understood better when examined in the context of matrilineal system. The woman is considered as *Ka Blei Iing* (goddess of the house). The mother ancestress (*Ka Iawbei*) is revered as one of the ancestral triad consisting of herself, her husband and her brother. The institution of *ka khadduh* (youngest daughter) is another aspect of Khasi matriliny. In traditional Khasi families each daughter is helped to set up her home by gifting her some land when she marries. The youngest daughter remains (even after marriage) in the house of her parents and becomes the custodian of family wealth and property. Khasi women enjoy considerable freedom in matters pertaining to themselves. She is free to choose her own husband; dowry and bride-price are unknown; divorce is permissible on grounds of barrenness and adultery and widows can marry again. Adultery is considered to be a serious offence. Women are not taken as sex objects but are parts of *ki kur ki jait* (matrilineal relations), *ki kha ki man* (relatives from the father's side) and *para Khasi khara* (the Khasi race), against whom any kind of assault would be sacriligious. Juanita War concludes by saying that women in the traditional society enjoy a high status and play significant roles in various spheres of life. They are regarded as important members of the socio-cultural and economic system. They, however, normally do not hold political and administrative offices. These are the domains of menfolk according to Khasi customs.

I.M. Syiem also maintains that perhaps in few societies are women so fortunate as in the matrilineal Khasi society and that the Khasi women have a distinctly higher position and status with greater responsibilities than women of other societies. Discussing the customary norms relating to the role of *Ka Khadduh*, the place of mother in family and society, marriage, divorce and widow-remarriage, adultery and the co-parcenary activities of women, Syiem says that women in Khasi society are not only treated as equal with men but in their social roles as mothers and custodians of religion and property, have an enviable place in society. The only area where the Khasi women have not played any role is the area of politics and administration. Today's society, however, is facing a change in family relationships, in attitudes and values even in kinship relationships. Conversion to Christianity, education, new work culture, urban living and contact with other cultures have given the women new options. Much of the traditional and religious practices in which the matrilineal kin group play a dominant role are no longer adhered to. Social interactions are less frequent. This has greatly weakened the effectiveness of the matrilineal kin group and has subtly affected the attitude and behaviour of the wife towards her kinsmen and her husband. She often suffers a conflict of loyalties. She is no longer regarded just as a kins-woman or a clan-woman. Her status is dependent on her own social position and that of her husband. Syiem concludes that Khasi women are joining the mainstream of larger society. In urban centres there is maximum exposure to and contact with other cultures. There seems to be a revaluation and rethinking in today's society. Khasi society is going through a state of change and adjustment and it naturally follows that there will be changes and adjustments in attitudes and social roles of women as they adapt to the times and the changing situation.

The traditional social and familial structures in Jaintia Hills are only local variations of what have been observed in Khasi Hills. For instance, as P.M. Passah points out, there is some variation in the residential pattern as compared to that followed in Khasi Hills. In Khasi Hills, the basic residential unit comprises of the mother, her husband and children whereas in Jaintia system the husband is not the member of the unit. He is only a visitor. In discussing women's role in traditional society, Passah says that in family life, in religious matters and in economic activities, women in Jaintia Hills have definite roles to play and occupy honorable positions in the society. The mother looks after all the domestic affairs of the society. In most cases, menfolk have been found to abide by the policy or decision of the mothers. Women are in overall control of household affairs. They are considered the founders of clans and religion; religious ceremonies at home are performed by women. Women thus occupy a position somewhat like that of a priestess. They also participate actively in economic activities. Such participation, Passah maintains, is very high among Jaintia women. As in Khasi Hills, the youngest daughter, *Ka Khadduh*, is the custodian of family wealth and property. Jaintia women, however, do not participate in political and administrative affairs which they feel are men's concern and profession. Passah says that women do not have any voting right in elections to traditional council and offices of the state. They are not allowed even to sit in any public council or *durbar*. Talking about the impact of education and Christianity, Passah maintains that although a change has taken place in the family structure when the husband became a part of his wife's family, the status of women remained unshaken. The spread of education and Christianity has not eroded the status of women in Jaintia culture. Although by a court decision during colonial rule, a change was brought in the status of the youngest daughter from being a mere custodian of family properties to having the right of title so as to enable her to dispose the property the way she likes. Other socio-economic roles of women, however, continue as the faith of the tribe in the matrilineal system is strong and rigid.

L.S. Gassah, however, maintains that though the inheritance of property and descent is followed in the mother's side, a woman is not bathed in the splendour of power. She is a much burdened individual. Matrilineal principle of descent and residence puts heavy responsibilities on the mother to ensure the welfare of the family. The dual loyalty that a man has towards his wife and children on the one hand and his sister's children on the other, sometimes contributes a feeling of insecurity in most women. Another distinct feature of women's role in social and family life can be seen where there is a pull between the avuncular and paternal authority. However, the woman, as the fountain head of a clan, is held in high respect. She occupies quite a distinct and respectful status in familial, social and economic spheres but are subject to certain restrictions so far as participation in political affairs is concerned. The birth of a female child is hailed for the simple reason of being sure of the continuity of the family and the clan. When she grows up, she is meticulously initiated and trained in adult responsibilities of keeping home. Women have also important roles to play in religious and economic affairs. Their status in the family in particular and the society in general are, therefore, respectable and distinguished. The spirit of freedom helps them to be active. However, in the present transitional phase, Gassah says, much changes have taken place which have tremendous effects on the society in general and the status of women in particular. The traditional pattern of family has changed. There are various other changes because of the impact of Christianity, education, new means of communication mobility of individuals, employment opportunities etc. Women had to adopt themselves to the changing environment. Gassah also points out that of late an enquiry into the matrilineal system of inheritance, descent and succession in general and status of both women and men in particular, is receiving attention in various circles. These issues are being debated seriously. One school of thought has even come out with a strong plea for an immediate changeover from matrilineal to patrilineal system. This school is concerned more about the status of men and the role they are expected to play rather than that of women.

In discussing the Status of Women in Garo Culture, Caroline Marak begins with reference to mythology. In Garo myths women occupy important position and enjoy so much respect that an insult to a woman could cause conflict and war. In legends women are portrayed as pure, beautiful, brave and noble. But in reality, Marak maintains, there is a subjugation of women. The matrilineal system does not protect their position and rights. Critically examining the customary laws, Marak points out instances when women suffer and are even subject to coercion. One such law is the law of *akim*. By this law, on the death of a spouse, a relative, – male or female as the case may be, – is to be given in marriage to the widow or the widower. When a suitable adult relative of the deceased is not found children are forced into marrying the much older survivor. Women are said to be the worst sufferers in such situations because when a girl refuses to be persuaded into marrying the widower by her male relatives (*chras*), coercion is resorted to. The female relatives of the girl have no say at all. Again, when a youngman is given in marriage to a widow with a daughter, the daughter is promised as his second wife. This custom is known as *dokchapa*. Thus it appears that even the matrilineal system has not adequately protected the position of Garo women. The mother is not the head of the family; she is required to obey her husband. Polygyny is practised with the consent of the principal wife and her *chras*. Though the woman inherits property, she does not wield exclusive right over it and her husband has the final word in exercising authority over household possessions as well as landed property. In the *mahari* or the body of the closely related members of a clan including those who have married into the clan, power rests with the males. Women have no voice at all. Even in the matters concerning women, their opinion is not sought or considered. They must always abide by the decision of the male members. Marriages are settled by the *mahari* and the opinion of the girl is not considered. The *mahari* can decide to give a very young girl in marriage to an elderly person and the girl has no redress. In the field of administration, women have no part. A woman can never become a village headman (*nokma*). She has also no role to play in religious ceremonies. The priest (*kamal*) is always a male. There is a sustained prejudice against women as reflected in such saying as, *Domok Wagam gri michik grisik gri* which means : *as a goat has no teeth, so a woman lacks brains.* Marak believes that from these impediments to their development Garo women were rescued to an extent by Christianity and education. In her assessment, education has brought about a revolution in women's world and their status. Economic independence that education has provided liberated her from tyranny and gave her self-esteem. They are in a better position than ever before to fight against prejudices, conservatism and double standards. In the last two decades women have come to the forefront of their community. Women's positive attitude is seen in their increasing participation in leadership and decision making at various levels. Even then, Marak asks, have the Garo women attained the status envisaged in the Constitution of India and her answer is negative because illiteracy is still rampant, ignorance hinders development and attitude of men has not changed much.

These assessments of the Khasi-Jaintia and Garo situations, presented by our contributors, are not claimed as complete and final. Many a vital questions might have remained unanswered. The seminar addressed itself to some of these questions, both empirical and conceptual, as has been reflected in the Report on the proceedings of the seminar appended to this volume. But our attempt at providing informations regarding both the traditional norms and the trends in the changing scenario seems to have been achieved in a large measure. The contributors deserve our sincere thanks. Their contributions will help in developing a comprehensive framework for studying the status and role of women in the matrilineal societal context of the Khasi-Jaintia and Garo Hills of Meghalya and how the matrilineal groups in these hills have reacted to the processes of change and have adopted to the changed and changing settings.

2

STATUS OF WOMEN IN TRADITIONAL KHASI CULTURE

Juanita War

Role differentiation and the status of women vis-a-vis men has always been an interesting subject of study. In recent times especially the subject is becoming more important because of the growing realisation and acknowledgement that women in many societies have been unduly suppressed. It can be said that in predominantly male-dominated societies women have been relegated to the status of second-class citizens. Secondly, the contributions of women to society have not been fully acknowledged. This is because traditionally women have been concerned only with hearth and home, and with the seemingly unimportant duties of cleaning, cooking, child-rearing and so on. Women in most societies are regarded as the weaker sex, not only in physical strength, but also in intellectual capability. As such, roles assigned to women have been restricted to the home, i.e., domestic roles. Perhaps a fact that needs assertion is that a society's stability and vitality can be maintained only if men and women play complementary roles, with equally important status in their own sphere of activities and domains. The loss of status, the indignity inflicted, and the supression of one sex by another create disharmony and imbalance in society. Thus practices and customs like female circumcision, bride/wife burning, ***devdasi, sati***, female foeticide etc., are decried by the more enlightened, because they indicate the brutal domination of one sex by another. Similarly, social aberrations like rape, sexual assaults and eve-teasing in the extreme forms are manifestations of a sick society. Where these are in the extreme, legislations and social reforms are needed to restore health and balance in society.

Societies differ because of factors like religion, the types of social and family organizations, social customs and practices. Different societies assign different status and roles to men and women. Tribal societies have customary laws and traditional practices which define the roles assigned to men and women in different ways. For example, in most societies in India 'women have no customary rights to land. Their rights are derived through kinship linkage to a male family landowner'.[1] It is maintained 'that there are few societies where women have retained a fast eroding customary rights over land, such as tribal societies of north-east of India'.[2] Similarly, social and family organisations in most tribal societies are such that there is greater freedom for women in terms of movement, choice of a life-partner, profession etc. Also, the in-built forces and mechanism to maintain social equality between men and women have remained intact for the most part. The numerical strength of such societies being lesser, it was necessary to maintain social cohesion and unity within the tribe. It was also equally important that both sexes contribute maximally to the maintenance and extension of the tribe. In the traditional Khasi society, for example, men were the warriors and protectors, the tillers of the soil, the hunters, administrators, priests etc. Their roles and duties were in domains outside the house. This is symbolised by the bow and arrow placed on a white cloth at the naming-ceremony of a baby boy. Women had the roles of mothers, housekeepers, custodians of family property, helpers in the fields and betel-nut and fruit groves. At the naming of a baby girl, the symbols for the roles she will play are *ka khoh* (sling basket) and *u star* (rope to carry the basket).

Role and status of women in traditional Khasi Culture

The uniqueness of the role and status of women in the traditional Khasi culture can be understood better when examined within the context of the matrilineal system practised by the Khasis. Descent is traced from the mother's side, and kinship is closer to the maternal side or the matrikin (*ki kur ki jait*) than to the paternal side (*ki kha ki man*). All the offsprings of the mother belong to the same *ing* (family) because they have the same *jait* (surname). By the same token, the mother, along with her children and grand-children, and her sisters, along with their children and garand - children, and their first cousins' families from the maternal side, constitute the *kpoh* (sub-clan). In other words, members of the same *kpoh* can trace their geneologies to a common mother ancestress (*Ka Iawbei*) . With the increase in the numbers of a *kpoh* when daughters and granddaughters marry, a new sub-clan can be created by splitting the existing branch. This is called *phiah kpoh* and is preceded by obtaining consent from the family council, followed by necessary rituals to seal the agreement. In such cases each daughter of the founding ancestress becomes the ancestral head of her own *kpoh* ; her daughters and granddaughters take after her original clan name. The process is repeated over generations as the clan and the tribe increases.

In the light of the traditional custom and practice of matriliny among the Khasis given in brief in the above statements, the status and role of women in the family and social organisations is very important. The woman is considered as *Ka Blei Ing* (goddess of the house) and *Ka Lukhimai* (the guardian spirit of the house). The names suggest not only the moral attributes of virtue, purity and goodness usually ascribed to woman, but also her role in the maintenance of the continuity and the growth of her family (*ing*), her subclan (*kpoh*) and her clan (*kur*). The mother ancestress *Ka Iawbei* is the source and fountainhead of all the family (*ing* and *kpoh*) members. The ancestress who had passed away long ago, was revered as one of the ancestral triad (consisting of herself, *Ka Iawbei*, her husband, *U Thawlang* and her brother (s), (*U Suidnia*) in rituals like *Ka Jingknia Ai-bam* when food was offered to the dead ancestors as tokens of remembrance and respect, and to seek their continued help and blessings for those family members still living in this world. One feature of Khasi matriliny is the closeness of the members of a *ing* (family) and *kpoh* (sub-clan). Thus a woman is 'mother' not only to her own children, but also to her sisters' children. To her nephews and nieces she is either *mei-san* ('grown' mother) or *mei-nah* (young mother) since they are also considered to be her own flesh and blood by virtue of their clan membership within the family. The rights and duties of the mother are extended to maternal aunts, and include control and authority related to the children's welfare or behaviour. The duties include taking care of her late sister's children and bringing them into her fold in the event of death. The woman has important decision-making powers along with her husband, her brothers, and other close family members. As *meirad* (maternal grandmother), the woman has important roles - as adviser in family affairs, as a moral instructor who teaches moral and social virtues, and as a source of life and being.

Matrilineal descent and unilineal kinship in the traditional Khasi culture does not mean a negation of the paternal side. In fact, patrilineal kinship (*ki kha ki man*) is an important part of Khasi life and culture. One aspect of the socio-cultural life of the Khasis is the recognition of the importance of the maternal and paternal sides in the creation and sustenance of life: the maternal side is the actual channel of life, and the paternal side gives life and stature; hence they are known as *ki longkha, ki nongai la ka longrynñieng*. Seen within this context, the woman as the paternal grandmother (*Mei-kha*) commands great respect because she is the mother of the father-progenitor. In many ceremonies, such as the naming-ceremony of a baby, the *Mei-kha* has certain privileges and important roles to play. Usually it is the *Mei-kha* or one of the *khas* (paternal aunts) who name the baby. Some customs and practices like *Ka leit nguh Mei-kha* (literally, 'to go and bowdown to the Mei-kha') signify great reverence and respect for the departed grandmother by her sons' children (*khun kha*). Similarly, paternal aunts, *ki kha*, are also given great respect because they are part of *ki longkha*.

The institution of *ka khadduh* (youngest daughter) is another aspect of Khasi matriliny. It was usual for traditional Khasi families to help each daughter to set up her home by gifting her some land when she marries. Since the last daughter is the one who remains in the house with the parents, she has to take charge of family properties. In other words, the *khadduh* becomes the custodian of family wealth and property, which in actual practice is controlled by elderly male members of the family i.e., the maternal uncles (*ki kñi*) and her brothers. The institution of *ka khadduh* includes some privileges and duties. Some of her duties as family treasurer were (1) to meet family expenditures for ceremonies (such as wedding, naming ceremony etc.) and rites (such as bone internment of dead relatives, religious rites etc.), (2) to look after family member(s) who have fallen into misfortune such as disability, the death of a husband or wife, divorce and so on, (3) to gather family members at the *ing-seng* (foundation house) for the various family affairs and rituals, (4) to look after the religion of the family, to prepare for the religious rites and assist her maternal uncles in the performance of the rites. In the Khasi matrilineal system, the youngest daughter of each family, in each generation succeeded to the office of custodianship over family property and religion. The name *ka iawbei khynraw* given to the *khadduh*, indicates the very privileged status, and the great responsibilities on her shoulders. More than the other sisters, *ka khadduh*, had the sacred duty to continue the family line through procreation, not only to pass on the family name, but also the office of *ka khadduh*. However, should a *khadduh* remain unmarried or has no female child, the youngest daughter of the next elder sister succeeded to the office.

Khasi matriliny with respect to land and power is a unique system. The *khadduh's* role as custodian of the family property indicates some access to the family wealth, especially for expenditures related to family affairs. However, she could not sell or dispose the ancestral property (*nongtymmen*) unless she had the consent of the family council consisting of her maternal uncles, her brothers, and her parents (if still living). Such cases were considered only in dire circumstances. Thus the *khadduh* had no absolute authority over land if this is part of the *nongtymmen* which must be handed on to the next generation. However, she and her sisters had access to, and control of, such land and wealth (in the form of gold, silver, corals, cash etc.) which had been given as personal shares or gift from the family self-acquired property (*nongkhynrawi*)', was entirely managed by the person (s) concerned, male or female. It appears that Khasi customary laws sanction same rights over land and hence give women access to 'the seats of decision-making and power'.[3] This is in contrast to the basic pattern of land inheritance which is 'patrilineal, controlled, owned and distributed by men to men'.[4]

Women's roles in the traditional Khasi society were not confined only to the house. They participated freely in socio-cultural functions, festivals and ceremonies. At ceremonial and seasonal dances (e.g. harvest dance) young un-married girls would bring out the best dance costumes of gold or silver crown, long and heavy gold necklaces, armlets and other jewellery worn over silk and brocade. The dances usually accentuate the purity and modesty of women. In the traditional culture women would not normally touch the rice beer used for different rituals, since women were supposed to maintain their honour (*burom*). Khasi women enjoyed considerable freedom in matters pertaining to themselves. In the area of marriage a Khasi girl was free to choose her own husband though the initiative should come from the boy in the form of courtship. If she liked him she would tell her parents and uncles of their desire to marry. This was followed by serious investigations from both sides to see if there is any relationship between the boy's and the girl's *kurs* (clans); if both sides were satisfied that any hint of incest (*ka sang*) does not exist, marriage would be negotiated. Another unique feature of the Khasi culture is that dowry or bride price were unknown; at the most the groom presents a bridal attire to his bride.

A man or a woman could divorce (*pyllait san shyieng*) on grounds such as barrenness and adultery, with the knowledge of the *kurs* of both sides. Adultery (*ka klim*) was a serious offence, since marriage between two individuals was also considered to be the *kur-kha* link between two clans. The concept of *ka klim* extended beyond this life; either partner could not re-marry until all rites and rituals related to the dead spouse have been observed, otherwise the surviving spouse was said to have committed *ka klim* if he or she re-married. In cases where either man or woman had committed adultery to the living or dead spouse, his or her family would perform a sacrifice (*jingkñia klim*) and the guilty party would have to pay for the expenditures. A monolith (*mawklim*) would be erected as a mute witness of the offence which had been observed. Widows in the traditional Khasi society could re-marry, usually a year after the death of her husband, and after she had returned the bones of her dead husband to his family and *kur* (clan) for internment in the clan ossuary (*mawbah*), and after she had completed all necessary rites. Then her relationship with his *kur* would remain cordial, even though she was free to form relationship with another *kur* through her second marriage. In the traditional Khasi society social interaction between the two sexes has always been open and free; platonic friendships could exist between boys and girls. Perhaps this accounts for the fact that rapes were extremely rare. Women were not regarded as sex objects to be used, but as part of the universal '*ki kur ki jait*' '*ki kha ki man*' (i.e., relatives from one's own clan and from the father's clan) or '*para khasi khara*' (belonging to the Khasi race), against whom any kind of sexual assault would be sacriligious. It was the duty and responsibility of a man to protect a woman's honour, not to violate it. The openness and free interactions between the two sexes have been mistaken by others coming from different cultural backgrounds as some kind of moral laxity. The fact is that pre-marital sex and adultery were considered to be serious social offences since the institution of marriage was considered sacred, a contract not only between two individuals, but between two *kurs*.

From times immemorial Khasi women were active participants in supplementing family income by tilling the soil, cultivation, looking after domestic animals, and such other occupations that did not require too much muscle power. In the Bhoi and Jaintia areas women spun thread from cotton and *endi* worms that they reared themselves, and wove clothes for the family. Women were also shrewd traders in the market places, selling fruits, vegetables, betel-nuts, and other products.

From the above observations it can be seen that women in the traditional Khasi society enjoyed a high status, and played their roles in the various spheres of life. There is however one area that is barred to Khasi women, and that is the area of political and administrative affairs. In the traditional Khasi culture, women could not participate in either village or state *durbar* since the Khasi tradition allowed only those with moustaches (i.e., mature men) to attend public meetings and take part in the deliberations. In other words youth, drunkards and women were debarred from the *durbars* at various levels (village, region, state). This could be due to the extremely difficult circumstances in the past when the Khasis were constantly at war with each other and with the neighbouring plains people. Issues discussed and decisions taken were those related to war, a subject in which women had no part. Secondly, Khasi *durbars* were serious affairs conducted with discipline, orderliness, decorum and propriety; any show of temper and irresponsible talk was not permitted.

Women could not normally hold offices of syiemship, sardarship, lyngdohship and wahdadarship (i.e., chieftainships at various levels). However, in the case of total absence of male heirs from a particular royal clan (*Syiem*), woman could also succeed to that position, as in the case of Ka Lar, *Syiem* (king or chief) of Nobo Sohphoh Syiemship. However, women had other functions within the state (*hima*). The mother or eldest sister or niece of the *syiem* usually became the *Syiem Sad*, symbolically the state priestess in the syiem's house, in charge of the preparations of the various rites and rituals related to the state; she also had other functions to perform. She was the keeper of the *syiem's* income and possessions; it was her duty to distribute them among the family members, including his wife and children.

Conclusion

In giving equality and some amount of freedom to women in the areas of marriage, widow's re-marriage, and the management of cash and property, the traditional Khasi society showed its regard for women as important members of the socio-cultural - economic system. This could be due to the type of matrilineal system practised by the Khasis. Jairamdas Doulatram, the ex-Governor of undivided Assam, had this to say: 'I sometimes feel that indirectly it (the matrilineal system) has considerable effect in encouraging the free progress of women and it tends to make them equal to men. Their innate qualities get scope for evolution and development and they are more mature members of their own society than are their sisters elsewhere'.[5] It could also be due to the tribalness of the Khasi society. Roy and Rizvi have stated that in tribal societies in the North-East 'there is greater freedom for women, higher literacy levels, greater mobility and higher participation in decision-making within the family and sometimes also in the village'.[6] Lastly, the unique status and position enjoyed by Khasi women could be a result of the inherent Khasi belief that all human beings are to be respected and honoured as fellow-beings. Disrespect and violence against any person - man, woman or child - would go against the basic tenet of the Khasi belief to earn righteousness (*ban kamai ia ka hok*). It would also be tantamount to disrespect for the person's entire clan (*kur*).

In conclusion, it must be stated here that many changes have taken place in the Khasi society. For example, the *khadduh* as the custodian and priestess of the family, has different roles and privileges in the present society. Since the scope of this paper is limited to a study of the traditional Khasi culture, it is hoped that it (the paper) has been able to throw some light on the unique and peculiar features of the status, position and roles of women in the traditional Khasi society.

REFERENCES

1. Roy, S. and Rizvi S.H.M., 'Power, Land and Woman', Paper presented in a *Seminar on the Status of Women in the Barak Valley* held at Karimganj, 26-27 November, 1988.

2. *Ibid.*

3. *Ibid*.

4. Agarwal, Bina, 'Who Sows? Who Reaps? Woman and Land Rights in India', *Journal of Peasant Studies*, U.K., July.1988.

5. See, Roy Hipshon, (Ed.) *Where lies the Soul of Our Race*, Shillong, Seng Khasi, 1982, p.4.

6. Roy and Rizvi, *opcit*.

3

WOMEN IN KHASI SOCIETY

I.M. Syiem.

Roughly half the world's population are women. There is no doubt about the fact that men and women are basically different from each other in their responses and perceptions, in their attitudes and world-view. Yet there is no denying the fact that in mental ability and achievement women deserve an equal status with men. For generations women have accepted soceity's placement of them. They had to conform to rules in a world where males dominate. Division of labour on the basis of biological (physical) difference probably had a lot to do with male attitude towards women. However, both men and women have their own place, a complementary part in the daily sphere of things. It is a kind of specialization that serves a very practical purpose. The so called Women's Liberation Movement mostly comes out of the fact that women's established work systems have been disturbed by birth control, and more time saving devices, giving them more leisure, higher education and a work need or economic necessity, besides a desire to raise their status in society. Too long they have been under male domination with no voice, no individual identity and no freedom to express their real selves and abilities. Now the women have access to the world of men. In 1918 they gained the right to vote.

Ever since they have proved themselves to be equally capable of achievements in every sphere of life outside the home.

Perhaps in few societies are women so fortunate as in matrilineal societies such as Khasi society. Khasi women have a distinctively higher position and status with greater responsibilities than women of other societies. They have greater liberty to express themselves. They are accepted and treated as individuals. They can, to a large extent, act independently. For instance, they can undertake any work jointly with their husbands or separately. Husband and wife infact have almost an equal status in the family. Even after marriage, each retains their respective clan's name. They also share equally in duties and responsibilities, as well as decision making, regarding matters concerning their home and children. It is only in matters outside the home that the males, the father or the maternal uncles, act as the representatives. Women's responsibilities and privileges are limitated to their families and their kinship group. Despite these limittions on their roles, women undoubtedly have a prominent and enviable position in Khasi society.

The Khasis trace descent through the women. Property is transmitted through women, notably the youngest daughter (*ka khadduh*). The children are affiliated at birth more intimately with the mother's relatives or kin group rather than the father's. In other words, the Khasis are a matrilineal people. Authority and control are in the hands of the maternal uncles and the father (*U Kpa*). It is not therefore, as is wrongly interpreted, a matriarchal society.

Undoubtedly the system allows a higher place for women than in most societies. The mother of the clan, *ka lawbei* (ancestress) through whom the lineage is traced, is highly revered. So are the maternal uncle (*U suidnia*) and the father (*U thawlang*).

The Khasi mother has special privileges and responsibilities in the home. She is not only the keeper of hearth and home but also has certain rights over house and property. These rights are sanctioned by customs and religious tradition. On her also depends the continuation of her lineage. If she is the *khadduh*, she is also responsible for the ancestral property (*ka nongtymmen*).

'She is also the one who prepares all the necessary items (*ki dah ki dong*) for rituals and hand over to the *Kñi* (maternal uncle) or to *Hymmen Rangbah* (Eldest brother) to conduct or to perform the actual rituals and to communicate with *U Blei* (Creator) for the prosperity of the clan and family'.[1]

Khasi religion, *Ka Niam Ing*, is essentially a family religion and it is more of a personal religious relationship with the family and the Creator. It is in this connection that the *khadduh* is often referred to as the family priestess which is not entirely correct. She only makes preparations for various religious ceremonies but it is her maternal uncle or brother who performs the actual rituals. The *khadduh* is referred to as the keeper of religion (*Ka bat ia ka niam*). Her house is *Ka Ing Niam*, a place of worship. In this respect, the woman's place in the home could be said to be not only a responsible one but also sacred.

Ancestral property (*Ka nongtymmen*) is transmitted through the *khadduh*. The *khadduh* has certain obligations and duties in her role as custodian of family property. She is not the heiress in the strict sense of the word. She does not have any control or rights to sell property without the consent and counsel of her maternal uncles and other siblings. The family property is more a joint family trust.

Much is expected of the *khadduh*. Her home is an open home, a refuge for the old and the needy, for any who are in distress among her kinsmen, her *kur* (clan). She cannot turn anyone away. She has a social obligation to fulfil towards them not only because she gets a major economic share but because she has to keep the honour of her *kur* (clan). It is a shame to have a begger for a kinsman. For this reason there were no beggars in the traditional society. Sometimes these kinship obligations place a heavy burden on the *khadduh* which she often finds difficult to fulfil if her resources are meagre.

The *khadduh* however, by virtue of her custodianship of ancestral property and her corresponding social obligations, has a unique status in Khasi society. She is more privileged among her sisters. She is the pivot, the cementing bond for family and clan relationships. She also has greater obligations to her *kur*. How far the *khadduh* has a say in the affairs of family and over property will greatly depend on her personality. Her husband usually does not interfere in matters of her *kur*, but he helps in the management of the property. The position of the *khadduh's* husband is slightly different from the other *nong kha*, the husbands of the other sisters due to the very fact that her position in her kinship group is different. Much has been said about the privileged position of the *khadduh* but little has been mentioned about the conflicts and strains she faces in her role, more particularly the conflict of loyalty to her *kur* and to her husband in areas of decision-making.

The role of the *khadduh* is changing in today's society. With conversion to Christianity, much of her traditional religious obligations in terms of *ka niam iing* and in bone internment ceremonies are no longer expected of her. They are, on the other hand, being replaced by other similar obligations. She is still expected however, to fulfil her social obligations towards her maternal kinsmen. She remains the central figure in the clan if not the only important one.

The sanction behind custodianship of property is customary. Increasingly the *khadduh* is claiming to be the sole heir to property with the right to sell it should she wish. There have been cases where disputes of this kind have been taken to court by the *kur*. The position of the *khadduh* is changing. She is going through a transitional period. She is still regarded as the traditional embodiment of the *kurla's* guardian of hearth and property. At the same time because relations may not be so close among siblings of a particular family, she may not evoke the same feelings of trust and devotion as before. Modern parents are now making use of the *will* system in dividing self-acquired property to minimise conflict. The major share usually still falls on the *khadduh* as is customary.

'It is from the woman that the clan springs'. The prayer or blessing invoked by the family is that she will multiply - *ban roi ka jait ka kynja, ban iar u tnum u tyndai*. In this aspect the woman is more than a child bearing asset. She is the custodian, the preserver of her clan, her family and her lineage. In her role of mother, the Khasi woman is not only revered by her maternal descendants but also has a special place as *ka meikha*, the father's mother. *Ka meikha*, during her life time and even after her death, is shown reverence by *ki khun kha* (her son's children). A new born baby is first taken to *ka meikha's* house for her blessings.[2] *Ka meikha* is present at the name giving ceremony (*ka jer khun*) of the baby and at most important events of the life cycle of her sons' families.

The Khasi social organisation is actually based on *ka tip kur ka tip kha* (the kinship system). Relatives on the father's side (paternal kinsmen) are respected and loved because they are *ki nongai ki nongsei rynieng* (the giver of life and stature). The maternal males on the other hand are looked upon as *ki nongbtin lynti, ki nongduai phirat bad ki nongsaid nongthew* (the guardians, the communicators, the diviners and the pleaders). *Ki kha* (paternal relatives) are recognised as the contributors of life to the individual. For this reason the woman from whom springs *U thawlang*, the father progenitor, the giver of life, has a high position in the society. Although her obligations towards her sons' children may be less she nevertheless has some special privileges.

Monogamous marriage is the norm in Khasi society as also the matrilocal residence. Marriage regulations include a careful scrutiny of *ka sang* (incest taboo) in this case referring to clan taboo and clan exogamy. The maternal males and *ki ksiang* (intermediaries) are usually involved in the social intricacies of arranging the match once the couple have agreed to marry. Usually the boy and his relatives instigate the marriage. Marriage is usually considered *Ka jutang*, a covenant, in the presence of God and man. Adultery (*klim kyrtep*) is frowned upon. Adultery, expecially by the woman, is taken very seriously by the clans concerned. The husband even has the right to inflict death on his erring wife if she is found guilty of the act. The husband will be encouraged and counselled by his kinsmen as well as by village elders to divorce an adulteress unless he chose to forgive her.

The adulteress demeans herself in the eyes of society by her act and she and her children suffer certain consequences. Her children for instance can no longer pay homage to *ka meikha*. After her death her bones will not be placed in the clan's *mawbah* (family tomb). There is certain stigma attached to the children of an adulteress but by no means are they considered to be illegitimate. They still bear the name of their lineage and their *kur* and although they are often considered as an embarrassment to the *kur* social and kinship relations are never completely severed. Only those who commit *ka sang* (clan taboo) are completely ostracised.

Divorce (*lait san shyieng*) and remarriage is permitted among the Khasis; the children remain with the woman and her *kur*. The unmarried mother has no stigma attached to her. The question of illigitimacy seldom arises because the children take their mother's name and belong to the mother's *kur*. If a woman remains a widow after her husband's death, she raises her children singlehandedly or with the help of her brothers or maternal uncles. She is respected and considered virtuous if she does the right thing. She and her children might even serve as examples to other families because of the hard work and sober living.

We have seen how important the woman is in her clan, her home and in preserving its religious and social unity. Because of the fact that the economic wealth of the family remains with the *khadduh*, Khasi women have been found to be as economically enterprising as men. They have been traditionally involved in economic activities, in trading and commercial ventures. This traditional trait is evident in the increasing number of women entrepreneurs engaged in private business in today's modern society.

Women also work in the fields side by side with the menfolk. They have their hands full with the household work besides eking out their livelihood. It is probably for this reason that there was no woman involved in state administration and the politics of the various Khasi states. They were debarred from attending the council or *durbar* of the states. They did not interfere in what they considered the business of men. The saying *Ynda kynih ka lar kynthei ka pyrthei ka la wai, lane lajot ka ling* (if the hen crows, the world, including the family, has changed for the worse) expresses traditional attitude about the limitations of women's roles. Khasi women were given more privileges and more responsible roles than their sisters in patrilineal societies. The basic male attitude of dominance and women's place however, cannot be denied although it is more overtly expressed. Men are still the protectors, the stronger (*U khadar bor u kiengwait u bah ryntieh*) and warriors. Deficiency in physical strength has always put limitations to certain roles of women in any society. Even in a matrilineal society, women are considered as the weaker of the sexes, to be cherished and protected.

When we take an overall view of the role and status of Khasi women in traditional society and a sum total of their privileges and corresponding duties we find that they have fared much better than their counterparts in patrilineal societies. They are not only treated as equal with men but in their social roles as mothers and custodians of religion and property, they have an enviable place in society. As *Ka Iawbei* (ancestress) and *Ka Meikha* (father's mother) they are revered. They have their matrilineal kinship group to support them, to sanction their roles, to retain their status in the society at large. In all aspects of social life they are accepted and respected for what they are, for their contribution to the solidarity of their kinship group and the society.

It is perhaps for this reason that the modern Khasi woman receives the same kind of respect whatever may be her job or status in society. This is evident in the way she is addressed as either *i mei* (mother) or *i kong* (sister).

All over the world women are encouraged and legally supported to step out from their homes to express themselves in various spheres of activity. Khasi women are also doing the same. They have distinguished themselves as teachers, both in schools and at the university level, as nurses and doctors, as engineers and architects, as administrators in state and Central services, as lawyers and magistrates and as entrepreneurs and business women. They have availed themselves of all the facilities in higher education and specialized fields. They have thrown themselves whole-heartedly in social works and social welfare programmes both in rural and urban centres.

There is significantly one area in which Khasi women have been slow in stepping forward, that is politics and the processes of legislation (*Ka synshar-khadar, ka sain hima-sima*), both at the district and at the state level. Traditionally they have not played much of a role in this area. There have been of course instances when in the absence of a male ruler or *syiem*, a woman was installed, for example, Ka Lar who was *Syiem* in the *hima* or the state of Nobosohphoh. In recent years women have played a role in supporting the political movements like the Hill state movement and in lobbying in their own way for one cause or another. But the women who actively entered the world of politics and in the business of law making were very few in number. Among them are Kong Mavis Dunn Lyngdoh who was a member of the Sadhullah government as early as 1937, and Kong Bonniely Khongmen who became a member of the Lok Sabha in 1952. Now there are Kong Maysalin War and Kong Maya Kyndiah.

It is however, surprising that a society which has emancipated women so much without their fighting for it, could produce so few women politicians. This may be due to the fact that it is hard for Khasi women to break the traditional norm. It is difficult for them to give their opinion in public, in an arena or platform which they had always conceeded as men's place. State activities were always considered as male activities (*Ka kam ki rangbah*). This is not to say that Khasi women are not qualified to stand for elections or are not involved or concerned in politics. They have expressed themselves through various political and non-political organizations and platforms. But they have been restrained by their traditional role to really venture publicly in this area. In recent times, however, we see a change of attitude and a growing desire on the part of women to be involved in politics.

There is also another area in which women have been tremendously supportive but have not really taken a leading role. Among Christians, there is not a single ordained woman pastor or deacons. As in traditional times, women take a secondary role. It is the men who lead in worship. This is not to say that women do not speak out on religious topics. They do, but only within a certain context, but never as pastors or priests.

The wife and mother in Khasi society serve as a link between her family of procreation, the (nuclear) unit of her husband and her children and her family of orientation, her natal matrilineal family. The maternal males exert a dominant influence in her life because of her role and position in the matrilineal kinship group. At the same time she is somebody's wife and she has obligations and duties to fulfill as wife and mother. The conflicts and strains are no doubt inherent in the traditional system but they are resolved due to the fact that the matrilineal group has precedence in the control over the woman and her children. Property binds her to her kinship group. Moreover, her husband has his own obligations towards his own matrilineal kinship group. There was mutual adjustment and understanding.

Today's society however is facing a change in family relationships, in attitudes and values even in kinship obligations. Coversion to Christianity, education, the new work culture and urban living and contact with other patrilineal cultures have given women new options.

In the family, decision making powers are being equally shared by husband and wife. The father is shouldering more responsibilities. In important events of the life cycle he is taking an increasingly active and important role in his own family. With conversion, much of the traditional and religious practices in which the matrilineal kin group play a dominant part are no longer adhered to. Social interactions are also becoming less frequent. This has greatly weakened the effectiveness of the maternal kin group and hence has subtly affected the attitude and behaviour of the wife towards her kinsmen and her husband. She often suffers a conflict of loyalties. She is no longer regarded just as a kins-woman or a clan's woman. Her status is dependent on her own social position and also in the status of her husband.

However, relationship has not changed radically from traditional relationship of equality among kinsmen and non-kinsmen. In work situations a woman, who has a high position, enjoys all the privileges which go with her office in terms of material benefits and respect. But outside work, in social situations, in marriages and deaths and other events, social relationships are just as cordial and friendly between a high placed official and perhaps a tea seller as it was earlier. All honest work is considered respectable by the Khasis. There is dignity of labour. There is no great discrimination as is evident in other societies.

A single working woman is recognised as having a status of her own both as a woman belonging to her *kur* and to her work. Unless the woman has a much higher position than her husband in terms of occupation she is usually recognised or accepted by her husband's position or status if she is married. At the same time women are considered and treated as equal; as persons in their own rights. They can assert their individuality without fear or men's domination or subjection. It is not just an attitude of tolerance. It is a traditional acceptance of women as individuals who can contribute meaningfully to the progress of the society. Nevertheless attitudes of male superiority is never totally absent.

Most modern husbands have a neutral attitude towards their wives' working. Earlier, as the need was not greatly felt, men preferred their wives to stay at home. Home was the women's place. Attitudes towards working wives have gradually changed. Of course in traditional society, women were allowed to work either independently or jointly with their husbands in any economic venture. The concept of work is however not the same as new spheres of work and work situations have opened up for women.

Research indicates that the greater number of women work because of economic necessity rather than for any other reason such as career or ambition or to achieve an independent status. Women work because they feel the need to supplement their husbands' income to make both ends meet. With more technological inventions and growing materialism it is an added incentive for both husband and wife to work in order to possess a few luxury items.

In other societies, working wives and mothers either face opposition or they are accepted rather grudgingly. Their household duties have not changed. The majority of husbands still expect their tired and working wives to serve them and the children as before. Khasi women receive more consideration from their men folk. There is a sharing of responsibilities, decision making and solving of problems. We have seen a similar pattern emerging in today's western industrialized societies. What is different in Khasi society is that this concept of mutual help and support and equal sharing of responsibilities have long been recognised and is rooted in the traditional system itself. Many working mothers experience role conflict and feelings of guilt. Their dual role in society is not willingly accepted or recognised. This conflict is less among Khasi because most husbands accept and treat their wives as social equals if not always as intellectual equals.

Among the working wives, most prefer teaching as a profession, or business for the main reason that it gives them more time for their families. Jobs that help them financially is acceptable. Khasi women generally are not competitive by nature. Probably this is due to the fact that they have no cause to really prove themselves or compete for anything. The system is such that it provides them economic and social security against poverty and need, against infidility and against the vagaries of human experience. Yet, to quote Nalini Natarajan, 'in spite of their high status, Khasi women were not aggressive but essentially feminine. While their movements were graceful and actions confident, oral traditions reveal that they had no air of superiority'.[2] it would not be complete however if we do not mention that in today's world, women, including Khasi women, are becoming increasingly competitive and aggressive in certain areas and situations. This is so as they become more aware of societal problems and are more knowledgeable about their rights and what they really want. Where men are more reluctant to push forward, women have not hesitated to take a stand, especially in what they consider important, in issues relating to morality, to the future of society, to social evils and undesirable elements in society. This happens everywhere including Khasi society. Most women are mothers at heart. Their world view and perspective are slightly different from men, however educated, qualified and rational they are. They carry the household mentality of cleaning up and arranging things to the larger society. Although, this may not be true of all women. For Khasi women, concern for home and concern for society springs from the same sense of responsibility and motivation. She is still the preserver and the custodian.

Khasi women are joining the mainstream of the larger society. In urban centres there is maximum exposure to, and contact with, other cultures. (They are thereby influenced by patrilineal view points (values), and attitudes). There seems to be a revaluation and rethinking in today's society on a number of issues having social significance, including the role of women. At the same time the individualistic ideology have affected sections of the women population and has given them a new perspective about themselves. Khasi society is going through a state of change and adjustment. It naturally follows that there will be similar changes and adjustment in attitudes and social roles of women as they adopt to the times and the changing situation.

REFERENCES

1. Synrem, H.K. *Revivalism in Khasi Society* (Doctoral thesis), 1986, unpublished.

2. *Ibid.*

3. Natarajan, N. *The Missionery among the Khasis.* Sterling Publishers Pvt. Ltd. New Delhi, 1977.

4

STATUS OF WOMEN IN JAINTIA CULTURE

L.S. Gassah

Women's status in Khasi-Jaintia society is not a new field of enquiry. There has been numerous studies already conducted both by local and non-local scholars. Even a cursory review of literature would lend support to this contention.[1]

Recently, a fairly good number of research works, articles, pamphlets and booklets have appeared providing new sources of information on the subject. Moreover, books on Khasi literature and poems, novels, etc., also contain informations about the status of men and women in the society. A series of serious articles have also appeared in a number of local language newspapers on the subject.

However, most of these studies do not deal directly with the status of women but there are discussions on the law of inheritance of property, descent, succession, the issue of matrilineal system etc., which may be useful in the study of the status of women and men in a matrilineal society.

Of late, enquiry into the matrilineal system of inheritance, descent and succession in general and the status of women and men in particular, is receiving more attention if one takes into account the views and concerns expressed through local newspapers, consultations, debates, researches, and seminars. It is an issue that is being debated seriously both at home and outside by people from almost all walks of life. It will not be out of place to mention here that one school of thought has even come out with a strong plea for an immediate change-over from matrilineal to patrilineal system of inheritance, descent and succession. This school of thought is concerned more about the status of men and the role they are expected to play in the society rather than that of women. Such debates seem to be natural in the transitional Khasi-Jaintia society which has already faced and is still facing the forces of change both in terms of its material and non-material culture. Needless to say, the academicians have an important role to play and contribute while exercising their minds and thought on this vast, complex, but topical issue at this juncture when the society is undergoing a rapid process of change.

Socio-Religious and Familial Role

The birth of a female child in a Jaintia society is hailed with a great joy. However, there is no discrimination in the upbringing of the male and female children. Both are treated equally although it may not be an exaggeration to say that parents often feel happier to have a female child than a male one for the simple reason of being sure of the continuity of the family and clan. No body would like to see their clan to face extinction due to the absence of a female child. A female child ensures the continuation of the family tree and saves such a family or clan from being looked down by others as an extinct one. As the female child grows up, she is meticulously initiated and trained into adult responsibilities of keeping the home.

Thus in the matrilineal Jaintia society the role and status of women, both in the family and the society at large, becomes different from that of other societies which do not follow the same system. Women in this society occupy quite a higher and distinct status only with certain restrictions especially in political affairs. As far as the domestic and household affairs are concerned, women have a distinct and significant role to play because they are duty-bound to take personal and extra-good care of their children as well as the other members of the family. Traditionally, the husband does not live with his wife and children. This, therefore, adds extra responsibility, or, in other words, the entire responsibility of looking after the overall welfare of the children and their upbringing rests in the hands of their mother.

Women in the traditional Jaintia society have an important role to play in religious and ritual ceremonies. Performing of ritual has also many things to do with matrilineal system. Thus, 'the mother is a person entrusted with the important duties of performing family rites and ceremonies, occupying the position of a family priestess, though in actual practice, males, who are her brothers, perform the actual task of sacrifice and other religious celebrations of the house. The mother prepares the necessary items of sacrifice among which are liquor (country made), special kind of bread, sacrificial animals, as well as various tools and instruments. But the actual task of sacrifice and the conduct of ceremonies is in the hands of men'.[2]

A woman, as the fountain head of a clan, is held in high respect. Virtue and purity are her essential attributes. Traditionally, no religious ceremonies are performed in marriage if a woman is no longer a virgin. Adultery is one of the most serious sins which a woman can commit. A husband, whose wife has committed adultery, is automatically separated from her. All social and religious connections between him and his clan and the woman concerned are snapped.[3] Moreover, it is considered a taboo according to the Jaintia custom that a woman should get married to a non-tribal or a person who embraces other religion different from that of the society. The children of that woman have no right or privilege whatsoever in any religious ceremonies and inheritance or property. After their death, their bones are never allowed to be kept in the same cromlech with other members of the clan. However, such a woman and her children can be accepted by the society and granted the usual rights if she leaves her husband and her children, their father. In that case she and her children are not treated as outcasts in the clan and the society.[4]

Women inherit properties; descent and residence are in their favour. The children belong to the mother and they remain under her custody in case of a separation or the death of the husband. A mother plays the role of the mediator in the family. Her status in the family in particular and the society in general is respectable and clearly distinguished. The Khasi-Jaintia usage ordains women to be loyal to their domestic duties, especially in the task of furthering family ties and affection. Simplicity in outlook, modesty in spirit, grace in movement are the general features of the Khasi-Jaintia maidens especially in the villages inspite of their position as land owners, property holders and business professionals. Added to these qualities, the spirit of freedom helps them to be active, healthy and thrifty.[5]

Economic Role

Jaintia women are not confined to household chores only. They contribute in many ways to the family wealth and income by engaging themselves in different economic activities. On account of their involvement and participation in various activities, in and outside their homes, it is obvious that their sphere of works and activities do not end within the four walls of the kitchen or their homes. They go out of the house to lend a helping hand to other members of the family in their agricultural and other productive activities. They are almost busy throughout the year both inside and outside their house.

In rural areas, shopping and marketing are done almost entirely by women folk. In olden days when road communication was absent and when goods were to be transported on headload, this activity was always performed by women. In winter seasons, when various kinds of fruits and vegetables are available in plenty, women are found to be busy transporting these items to the markets for sale. They come back home from the market with their conical bamboo baskets full of daily essential things, like rice, fish (both fresh and dried), salt, sugar, onion, oil, etc., for the family consumption. In the War area of Jaintia Hills, women are seen at least twice a week (that is on every market day and two days after that) with their baskets filled to the brim with betel-leaves, hurrying towards the market place to sell their goods. Betel-nut or areca-nut is also carried on headload by men and women on market days for sell. In the War area, where betel-leaf cultivation is so predominant, the services of both men and women are required. Plucking of the leaves is, however, the men's job. Women do the work of assembling the leaves meticulously in a neat and tidy way into small bundles for sale in the market. Nowadays, due to improved road communication, these items are transported by bus, but the traditional way of transporting them by headload is still continuing.

Women in the Jaintia society have a large number of responsibilities to perform. They look after the hearth and kitchen, lock up and set free the cattle and sheep before they are taken out by their elder children or other boys engaged to look after the cattle. Women help in raising crops and vegetables including kitchen gardening, in practising professions, trades and so on.[6] In respect of undertaking trade and commerce, no restriction is imposed on the women; they are free to practice such profession so as to help raising the family income. Generally, the Jaintia women are very good in trade and commerce. Against this background, women in the society are therefore to be seen busy in their homes, in the fields, either in *jhum* or wet-rice cultivation, and in the market places. Women work and move freely in all these places without any inhibition.

Political Role

Women of the Jaintia society, though occupying a distinctly higher status in social and economic sphere, are subject to certain restrictions so far as participation in political affairs is concerned. Traditionally, in political matters, a woman does not have any role to play and she is not allowed to participate in political decision-making process. Women are not allowed to attend any *durbar* or council. They are not given the right to speak or attend any public meeting which concerned the political affairs of either a village or *elaka* or *hima* (state). It is a taboo to see women in a political platform. According to traditional custom, they are not given the right to vote in any election to the offices of the traditional Chiefs. We therefore came across many tenets which speak about the misfortune or bad days waiting ahead if a woman takes in any form of political activity. Deliberations and decisions, planning, administration and policy-framing, and the burdens of management belong to the man.[7] Thus as far as political affairs and activities are concerned, women are devoid of any rights and position. However, it is not out of place to mention here that there are stories and legends in the Jaintia society which mention about the existence of women rulers. Reference may be made to the legend of *Ka Syiem Latympang* who established her own kingdom and ruled over her people. She was quite powerful and wise.[8] Thus, although political affairs were dominated by men, the society had "occasionally" produced such able rulers among women too.

Property : Rules of Inheritance

Women inherit properties. Sometimes, the youngest son may also inherit ancestral properties. However, a Jaintia man cannot be said to be a man without any property. Normally he has no right over ancestral properties, but he can have self-acquired property or *yutran*.[9]

One of the opinions with regard to the rule of inheritances of property in the Khasi-Jaintia society is that it is purely matrilineal in organisation. Property is of two kinds – inalienable and alienable.[10] The former is called *yongrim* or ancestral and the latter is *yutran*, that is, personal. Inheritance is generally on the female side, except in the case of the Bhois and the Biates. Inheritance of ancestral property passes from the mother to the youngest daughter, *ka khadduh* or *ka khynruit* or *ka yang-yung*. If the youngest daughter dies, the property is inherited by the next youngest daughter in point of age. If no successor is available from the family, *ka yung*, or *ka kur* or *ka kpoh*, then the family has to look for the nearest branch starting again from the youngest daughter of the next family. If there is no daughter at all in the family, then the youngest son succeeds. Only when the family successors are extinct (*duhjait*), the system of adoption (*rap-yung*) is resorted to. Ancestral property cannot be alienated without the consent of all the possible heirs of the whole family.[11]

Discussion on the rules of inheritance of property as well as the status of women in Jaintia society will not be complete without making a reference to the role-status of the youngest daughter or *ka khadduh*. While the elder daughters set up separate households a few years after their marriage, the youngest daughter continues to stay in the mother's house. She has to shoulder multifarious responsibilities in looking after her parents, mother's brothers, married/unmarried brothers and sisters. If any member of the family is widowed, divorced or fall into any misfortune, it is the duty of the youngest daughter to look after them and to give them shelter if the need arises. The house of the youngest daughter is a refuge to the members of the matrikin in case of a contingency.

The youngest daughter, although inherits the ancestral property, is not free to deal with it as she pleases. Each and every move she makes should be within the knowledge and with the consent of her brothers or the mother. She is merely the custodian of the property while real control over them is vested in the hands of her male matrikin.[12] Against this background, it is therefore opined that 'no one actually inherits property in the Jaintia traditional custom. What the members of the family get is not inheritance but a share. The share of women is to act as custodians of the property, and the men's share is to manage that property. The house of the youngest daughter is a place where all the shares are brought together. This custom was so arranged that any member of the family who is in difficulty will always be given shelter and protection in the youngest daughter's home'.[13]

Changes

Though the inheritance of property and descent is followed in the mother's side, woman of the society is not bathed in the splendour of power. She is a much burdened individual. By dint of the matrilineal principle of descent and residence, heavy responsibilities are laid upon the mother to ensure the welfare of the family. The matrilineal sytsem of descent not only put full responsibility upon the mother to bring up her children, but the dual loyalty that the man has towards his wife and children on the one hand and sister's children on the other, sometimes contributes a feeling of insecurity in most women which make them feel that they must be economically independent so that in the failure of the male members to provide for them, they can be assured of a livelihood.[14] Another distinct feature of women's role in social and family life could be seen where there is a pull between the avuncular and paternal authority. The emergence of the mother figure as a dominant personality is clearly observed in this matter.[15]

In the transitional society, like the Jaintia society, much changes have taken place. These changes have tremendous effects on the society in general and the status of women in particular. The traditional pattern of family has changed from what it used to be. There are many factors responsible for this; for example, the impact of Christianity, Education, means of Communications, mobility of individuals due to employment or in search of jobs, etc. Women of the society have to adapt themselves to this changing environment. They take up different vocations in different fields. Some had even tried their hands in politics but as ill-luck would have it, none could as yet come out successful.

REFERENCES

1. Mention may be made of a few of the published works like:

   (i) P.R. Mawthoh: *Balei U Khasi Um Roi Spah* (Glimpses of the Socio-Economic Drawbacks of the Khasi), 1967.

   (ii) A.S. Khongphai: *Ka Shongkha Shongman, Longkha Longman* (Marriage and Family), 1971.

   (iii) A.S. Khongphai: *Principles of Khasi Law.*

   (iv) B. Thangkkhiew: *Ka Ain Jong ka Spah Hiarpateng etc.* (Law of Inheritance of Property etc.), 1973.

   (v) K. Rapthap: *Khyllie Pat Parari Ia ka Khasi - Pateng* (An Appeal for Economic Revival), 1978.

(vi) K. Rapthap: *La Shaiong ki Khasi Ngain* (Cloud Hovers over the Khasis), 1978.

(vii) Eldon Rapthap: *Ka Jingpynthymmai Ia ki Rukom Khasi* (The Need to Revive Khasi Customs), 1979.

(viii) J.D. Stone Lyngdoh: *I Thymmei Ka Long-bynriew* (Socio-Economic Conspectus of the Khasi-Pnar), 1979.

2. Bareh, Hamlet *The History and Culture of the Khasi People*, Shillong: Author, 1967, p. 321.

3. See Singh, Kynpham 'Khasi and Jaintia Religion', in *Khasi Heritage* (Ed) Hipshon Roy, Shillong: Seng Khasi, 1969, p. 102.

4. Pakem, B. 'Ki Riti-Dustr Jong Ka Jaidbynriew Pnar' (Customary Laws of the Pnar Society), Seminar paper on the occasion of "The International Year of the Youth". Jowai : Youth Organisation of the Presbyterian Church, 1985.

5. Bareh, Hamlet. *op. cit.* p. 339.

6. *Ibid.*

7. Singh, Kynpham. 'Syiem and Durbars In Khasi Polity', *Tribal Institutions of Meghalaya* - (Ed) S.K. Chattopadhyay, Guwahati : Spectrum, 1985, p. 14.

8. Lyngdoh, U Homiwell *Ki Syiem Khasi Bad Synteng*, Shillong : Author, 1952, pp. 12-15.

9. Pakem, B. 'The Jaintia Tribe of Meghalaya', Paper in a Seminar on Social and Political Institutions of the Hill People of North-East India, Shillong: NEICSSR, 1977.

10. Bareh, Hamlet. *op. cit.* p. 329.

11. Pakem, B. *op. cit.* (note 8)

12. *Ibid.*

13. Pakem, B. *op. cit.* (note 3).

14. See also Nongbri, Tiplut. 'Problems of Matriliny: A Short Review of the Khasi Kinship Structure', *NEICSSR Journal*, Vol. 8 No. I April 1984, Shillong, p. 9.

15. *Ibid.* p. 8.

5

STATUS OF WOMEN IN JAINTIA SOCIETY AND CULTURE

P.M. Passah

The women throughout the world are still beset with age-old problems of discrimination and exploitation. Yet society is still hypocritical in its attitude towards women. Today, inspite of all the talks, conferences, demonstrations, protests, legislations, and above all, the declaration of the International Year for Women of the World in 1975 by the United Nations, the world profile of women is still depressing. Of late, widow-burning was sought to be revived in India although it was outlawed since 1829 by Lord William Bentinck. As against this grim-world of women, it would be interesting to examine the status of women in one of the matrilineal societies of Meghalaya, the home of the three matrilineal tribes - the Khasis, the Garos and the Jaintias. We propose to consider here the status of women in the Jaintia Society.

Under the matrilineal system, the Jaintias like their brethren the Khasis, reckon their descent through the female line. The children take the name of their mother's clan, are members of her lineage and clan, and live in her social group. But there is some variation in the residential pattern followed according to the traditional Jaintia custom as compared to what being followed among the

Khasis and the Garos. While among the Khasi and Garo societies, the basic residential unit comprises of the mother, her husband and the children; in the traditional Jaintia Society, the husband is not the member of the unit. The husband is like a stranger in his wife's house and can hardly interfere in the family matters of her clan. It is his brothers-in-law and the uncles of the wife who play the vital role in his wife's family matters. The husband only visits his wife at night and generally leaves her house at dawn. But among the educated and christian families, a change has taken place where the husband becomes part of his wife's family.

This paper is an attempt, as already stated above, to examine the status of women in the Jaintia society. Being a member of the tribe, the author gives here an insider's point of view on the issues concerning the role of women in the Jaintia culture.

Women's Role in the Traditional Society

In this section we will examine the role of women in the traditional society with respect to the family life, religious matters, economic activities, social life, and political activities.

The Family Life

The matrilineal system signifies great reverence and respect to motherhood. True to the matrilineal principle, the Jaintia woman occupies an honourable position in the society. The mother of a family looks after all the domestic affairs of the family. The role of her brothers and uncles is that of the supporters and bread-winners of the family. Man seldom cares to know about the daily needs of the family although he works hard to earn as much as possible for providing all those needs of the family and for saving the surplus. On the other hand, the mother plays a vital role in rearing, training, and educating her children.

In most cases, the menfolk have been found to abide by the policy or decision taken by the mothers in so far as the domestic affairs are concerned. It is usually considered that it is not the concern of a man to do any shopping and any other household chores. Rather, women would consider it a *taboo* for a man to hold a broomstick and clean the house. He has to provide the family finance no doubt but it is none of his business to bother about the domestic affairs. Women are in overall control of household affairs of the family and men should not interfere with what the women decide in this respect. Menfolk would figure only in the making of decisions on crucial matters like buying and selling of movable and immovable properties, cultivation, trade and business.

In most parts of Jaintia Hills as was in the plain areas of the erstwhile Jaintia Kingdom, the people were and still are practising sedentary system of cultivation which began since time immemorial. Hence the Jaintia families did have landed properties for wet paddy cultivation and movable properties like gold and silver ornaments and livestocks. However women's consent used to be taken while disposing such properties by their menfolk.

Religious Matters

In the matrilineal society, women are considered the founders of clans and religion. Among the Jaintias, religious ceremonies at home are in the hands of the women. They perform the sacred duty of making preparations for offering sacrificial food to the departed souls of their ancestors. The sacrificial food is called *I Siang I Pha*. The traditional belief of the Jaintias is that the souls of the dead live on in heaven and are believed to visit occasionally their families on earth. The women are thus occupying a position somewhat like that of a priestess. Therefore the women are the administrators as well as the priestesses in their own homes. The uncles and other male members of the family perform the religious rites outside the home. The women also receive the bones or ashes of the dead after they have been collected by men when cremation is over. This ceremonial function performed by women is known as *I Piam Chyieñ*. Similarly the ashes of the members of the family who died anywhere away from home would be brought and received by the women in the ancestral house called *I Yung Blai*. This ritual ceremony is called *I Rah Chyieñ*.

The Jaintias do have their priests and priestesses who perform religious rites and ceremonies for the community particularly during their most important national festival known as *I Beh Dieñkhlam*. It may be noted here that a woman who got married to a non-Khasi or a non-Jaintia will lose her religious connection with her family at the time of her death when her ashes or bones would be kept outside the family cairn (tombstones). Her children too would lose the right of inheritance to property and participation in religious rites and ceremonies.

Economic Activities

The Jaintia women do not only play a great role in domestic and religious affairs but they also participate actively in economic activities as well. The female work-participation is very high among the Jaintia women. They are as strong and energetic as men and can work in cultivation and itinerary trade and business just like menfolk. But they do not get equal wages for equal work. In certain cases, women are using a spade as big and heavy as the one used by men in wet cultivation. Women can also carry heavy loads on their backs up and down the hills. A pregnant woman normally continues to work manually even till the advanced stage of her pregnancy and there have been cases where a child was born in the farm, in the market place or on way to or from the market place.

The high female work-participation may be accounted for by the heavy economic burden on the males. According to the Indian Census report, more than 40 per cent of the Jaintia population is under the age of 15 years. Thus the economic burden of the productive males has to be lessened by the high level participation of women in economic activities. Besides participating actively in economic activities, women also enjoy the property rights to the exclusion of men in tune with the matrilineal system. Under this system, inheritance of property passes from the mother to her youngest daughter known by different names (e.g. *Ka Khadduh*, or *Ka Wasdiah*, or *Ka Wakham*) in different places in the Jaintia Hills. In case of death of the youngest daughter leaving behind no child of her own, the youngest among her sisters whom she had predeceased, would substitute her and inherit her mother's ancestral property. In the event of there being no daughter at all in the family, an heiress has to be found out from the nearest kin of the family who would inherit the ancestral property. But the personal or self-acquired property of the mother would be jointly inherited by the sons if their number is more than one.

The traditional matrilineal system does provide motivation for entrepreneurship among the agates (non-heiress).[1] Thus women participation in employment and business activities is very much on the high side.

It must be added here that it is wrong to think that the youngest daughter inherits the property in the legal sense. She is only the custodian of the properties to be managed, maintained, and controlled by her uncles and after them, by her brothers. The ancestral house is under occupation and all members of the family will have a common use of the family properties. In times of bereavement or performance of religious rites and sacrifices, the youngest daughter will have to defray all the expenses necessary out of the family wealth and property. The visiting husbands do give a token contribution like baby food for their newly born child and clothes for their wives. But they do not have much economic obligations and responsibilities in bringing up their children.

Social Life

As is the case with all hill tribes, there is no caste or class system among the Jaintias. It is usual for a poor woman to get married with a wealthy man and *vice versa*. The Jaintia women have full freedom to choose their own life partners and to re-marry after widowhood. Divorce is not uncommon. However no child can be an illegitimate child even if the child is born to a woman from the husband with whom she was not formally married. Marriage within the same clan is a great sin regarded as *I Wasang* and the couple who dare commit such mistake would be both punished and driven out of the Jaintia society.

Unmarried women are very much respected. They continue to live in the ancestral house and participate fully as any other married women in the family affairs. An unmarried woman used to be given the highest respect at the time of her death when special ceremonies known as *I Thang Sati* were held during her funeral. Women are also the well-dressed members in the family. Whenever a baby girl is born, the mother and her family would think of making provision for her gold or silver earings and other ornaments. In ordinary times, women may put on ordinary dresses but in special occasions they would put on what they called a *ryndia* or a *muka* or a *dhara* dresses. In matter of child rearing, there is no differential treatment of the male and female children. In other matters the attitude may vary from family to family.

Political Sphere

The Jaintia women consider politics as being men's concern and profession. This consideration emanates from the fact that in the past men alone could fight and defend the home or the country from an enemy. Therefore men should organise and administer public affairs so as to ensure peace and security. Men of course, considering the weaker sex as being unable to rule and administer public affairs, do not allow women even to sit in any public council or durbar. Women do not have any voting right in elections to traditional council or offices of the state.

Men consider that women are concerned with domestic affairs and should not dabble with public affairs. The women too accept this position generally. It may thus be noted here that both men and women have mutual respect for each other and recognise their respective responsibilities in spheres clearly demarcated. But in view of their active participation in domestic and religious affairs as well as in socio-economic life, women need not necessarily occupy state or political offices. They do have a great part to play in politics when they are fully active in all other aspects of life. And, there were indeed instances of Jaintia women rulers. Mention may be made of *Ka Piang Sariang*, a legendary woman ruler and the Queen *Latympang*. There are also references in *Jamini Bharata* and *Raja Tarangini* to the women kingdom variously referred to as *Nari Rajya* or *Promila Rajya* or *Stri Rajya* that ruled the Jaintias in ancient times. But conclusive proof in this regard is yet to be made.

Impact of Education and Christianity

We have said earlier that among the educated and christian families, a change has taken place where the husband becomes part of his wife's family. Yet the status and the role of women become either more manifested or remain as they were before. Christianity has not been able to transform the traditional custom of matrilineal descent and inheritance. In the domestic domain, women control and administer the household affairs as usual. While women hold men in high esteem by not allowing them to do shopping, to wash their clothes, to cook, to draw water from the well, to touch a broom-stick or to clean a house, men respect women for the sake of their womanhood and modesty and allow them a free hand in the domestic affairs. The sisters and the cousins are cooperating with one another in order to see that men have not to bother themselves with the household chores. This spirit of cooperation and mutual help among sisters and cousins however appears to have been on the wane now and whenever a woman falls sick or is in confinement, her husband has to take full responsibilities in looking after the household affairs. Nuclear families have come into existence both among christian and traditional families and the husbands have taken full responsibility in bringing up their children.

Women also have full freedom to participate in church affairs. This is particularly true with the Presbyterian Church which is the biggest and well-organised church in Jaintia Hills. The women's wing of the churches is equally strong in their organisation as the general congregation which men control and administer. The women play a vital role in mobilising finances either for the requirement of the local church or for the requirement at the different levels of the church organisation.

The social status of women remained unshaken. It has rather become more secure as divorce is very much discouraged by the churches. Similar is the case with the educated women within the traditional families. But educated women have learned how to avoid manual work. They have been enabled to do so because they can now choose their work including government services where conditions are more suitable for women. This means women still contribute to share the economic burden of menfolk.

The spread of education and christianity has not eroded the status of women in the Jaintia culture. But the

British rulers did bring about a change through court decisions in the status of the youngest daughter from being a mere custodian of the family properties to having the right of title so as to be enable her to dispose the property the way she likes. Other socio-economic roles of women in the Jaintia society, however, continue as the faith of the tribe in the matrilineal system is strong and rigid. But the women can now enjoy the voting right under the Indian Constitution although they are still precluded from participating in the election of traditional chiefs. They do, however, actively play behind-the-scene politics. They have not been entirely excluded from political processes.

Conclusion

The Jaintia society, following the matrilineal system, has unique features of culture and tradition. Its social system with emphasis on matrilineal family structure has a built-in mechanism to favour women .with property rights and family responsibility. The birth of a baby girl is a happy occasion. According to the Census of India Report 1971, there were more females than males among the Jaintias up to 1921. But since 1931, the sex-ratio fell down and by 1971 it was 958 per 1000 males in rural areas as against the total of 942 in the whole district. This is insignificant.

The Census of India Report 1971 explained the dispartiy (i.e. sex ratio) in the Indian population as due to four factors, viz., (i) Female infanticide, (ii) Neglect of female infant life, (iii) Premature co-habitation and child bearing, and (iv) Low population of the females. While the first factor is unthinkable, the second and the fourth factors are far from truth in the case of the Jaintia society and culture. The third is the only real factor which has been responsible for greater mortality of women in child birth leading to some disparity in the Jaintia population in recent years in favour of males although it may be insignificant.

The Indian Constitution recognises equal rights and opportunities for women in the society. The Jaintia women have already been enjoying a greater status and role since long in social life except in active politics. Now they are, however, free to participate in politics if they want. In recent time there was an instance of a woman who was nominated as a member of the Jaintia Hills Autonomous District Council. If therefore, the Jaintias were to claim equal rights to property under the matrilineal system, it is for men to stake their claim. The passing of the *Meghalaya Succession to Self-Acquired Property (Khasi and Jaintia Special Provision) Act 1984* has paved the way for the Jaintia parents to distribute at least their self-acquired property to sons.

REFERENCE

1. For a detailed study, see P.M. Passah, 'Inheritance among Matrilineal Tribes of North-Eastern Region of India: Its Socio-Economic Implications and Evolution', *Vision* (Journal of the Institute of Economics and Social Studies, Bhubaneswar, India), Vol. VII, No. 3 & 4, January - June 1988.

6

STATUS OF WOMEN IN GARO CULTURE

Caroline R. Marak

To start with a reference to Garo mythology seems appropriate as the myths might express the concept of woman among the tribe besides explaining natural phenomena. In the mythology handed down from time immemorial by our forefathers to the present generation and recorded in the recent period by a few Garo authors from the narrations of bards from all over the land inhabited by the Garos, woman occupies an important position and figures frequently in the tales. *Nostu Nopantu*, a goddess, is said to have given birth to the earth in the sense that she gave shape to it. It was *Tatara Rabuga*, the supreme god in the Garo pantheon, who had created the earth, but the earth lay buried under the dark, deep water. As the earth had not hardened and the level of water had not been limited to a certain point, so *Nostu Nopantu* asked the father of Apit and Ago to sow the seeds of cliffs and grains of plaranx. When the seeds of stone grew big to form cliffs and precipices, land was raised and clefts formed on its sides, so that the water flowed away and collected on one side of the land. The same goddess then asked the sisters Tikre and Tikse to sow the living grains and seeds of various trees, grass and weeds. Thus the mother earth was clothed in green.

Another goddess gave birth to animals of the land and of the water; she also gave birth to the sun, to the god *Misi Susime*, to spirits, and lastly, to fire. While giving birth to fire she died. At her cremation, a buffalo brought to be killed escaped; as it bounded away its foot prints became the Milky Way. Her funeral pyre became the Square of Regasus and the pole used for carrying her body to the pyre was turned into the Belt of Orion.

Wangala, the most important traditional festival of the Garos, owes its origin to an extremely poor widow called *Ae* whose pure and untainted heart and whose act of burning incense to welcome the stranger, the god *Misi Saljong*, won the blessings of the latter.

In the myths women enjoy so much respect that an insult to a woman can cause conflict and war. In legends women are portrayed as pure, beautiful, brave and noble and faithful wives. In the history of the tribe women figure prominently though they did not assume leadership during the course of their wanderings from Tibet to their present homeland. They lent active support to menfolk in their numerous conflicts and at times they took part in warfare. Women are also respected as progenitresses of the clans of the tribe.

Coming to the reality from the world of mythology and legends brings one into contact with more facts and details about the status of the woman. From a study of the traditional oral history it appears that matriliny was practised by the tribe since the distant past.

Women in the Traditional Society

System of matriliny as practised by the Garos has been analysed by Dr. D.N. Majumdar as follows: 'The hallmark of the Garo society is matriliny. Matriliny permeates the whole society; descent is matrilineal, inheritance is through the females, residence after marriage is uxorilocal, and so on.. Clan affiliation among the Garos is determined through the mother and paternal line is almost ignored in their kinship system. .... The matrilineal kinship system of the Garos has given rise to a structure of joint families based on uxorilocal residence. Garo lineages are based on traceable blood relationship through female and Garo clans are based on the belief that all members of the clan are related through blood in the female line. In Garo society the kinship group is the basic group which can be considered as the unit of intimate social, economic and to some extent, political relationship. ... The Garos select one of their daughters (not necessarily the youngest or the eldest) to be the inheritress. The daughter nominated by the parents to be the inheritress is to stay permanently in the parental household after her marriage and thus, she, along with her husband, is expected to look after the property as well as the parents in their old age. As the inheritress is a member of her mother's lineage and as the father belongs to an entirely different lineage, it is necessary that the resident son-in-law belongs to the principal male of the household's lineage, preferably a close relation of his. This has given rise to the system of bringing one's own sister's son as the resident son-in-law of the household. After the death of the older couple, the younger couple inherits the property of the household and thus becomes the owner of the household.'[1]

This system of bringing in the husband's nephew into the household as the resident son-in-law to continue the male lineage is known as the law of *Akim*. By this law, on the death of a spouse, a relative – male or female as the case may be – is to be given in marriage to the widow or the widower. This law affects both men and women adversely. When a suitable adult relative of the deceased is not found children are forced into marrying the much older survivor. Women may be said to be the worst sufferers in such situations because when a girl refuses to be persuaded into marrying the widower by her *chras* or male relatives coersion is resorted to which always takes the form of beating. On the question of compulsion, the female relatives of the girl have no say at all; they allow the custom to take its course without considering its merit, and remain silent spectators. This custom has been in practice in urban as well as rural areas, among the educated as well as the illiterate. In Tura town in 1957, on the night before her sister's funeral, a girl of twelve was subjected to about five hours of 'questioning' and persuasion until under the threat of beating, she agreed to marry her brother-in-law.

When a young man is given in marriage to a widow with a daughter to succeed his deceased male relative, the daughter is promised as his second wife. This custom of giving the daughter of the first marriage as second wife is known as *dokchapa*. This custom is still in practice among the non-christians. The reason for the continuation of this atrocious custom is ignorance. Those who still practise it do not feel that it is wrong or against all norms of morality. They explain it away saying that their ancestors had practised it and thus the custom has acquired the sanctity of traditional law. However, the 1980's have seen the law of *Akim* become increasingly weak and today even in the interior villages women usually choose whom they like and cannot be forced to replace their deceased sisters. The weakening of traditional custom is due to the spread of education among women.

Though a Garo woman's status is normally expected to be much better than that of her sisters in patrilineal and patriarchal societies, her position has not been favourably affected by the matrilineal system. Power rests with the males and the *mahari* or the closely related members of a clan including those who married into the clan. The mother is not the head of the family; she is required to obey and respect her husband. Though women inherits property, she does not wield exclusive right over it and her husband has the final word in exercising authority over household possessions as well as landed property. There are instances when a *nokkrom* or resident son-in-law squanders the family possession and property and ruins the family while his wife remains a dumb spectator. When a husband beats his wife, nobody objects; but when a wife beats her husband, it is considered a serious offence. Polygyny is practised with the consent of the principal wife and her *chras*.

The fact that the Garo women have no voice in determining their own fate has been stated by Dr. D.N. Majumdar thus: 'In the affairs of the *mahari* the women have no voice at all. Such matters are decided exclusively by the male elders. ....And as males do not consider the opinion of women in such matters necessary, there is no way for the women to influence the *mahari* affairs, except through their husbands. Even regarding matters concerning women, the opinion of the woman concerned or all the women in general of the *mahari* is not considered as essential. Women must always abide by the decision of the male elders. Marriages are settled by the *mahari* and the opinion of the girl is not considered significant. The *mahari* can decide to give a very young girl in marriage to an elderly person, and the girl has no redress.'[2]

The position of the *nokna* or the heiress of the *aking* which means a large area of land belonging to a particular clan, is hardly any better. On her behalf the land is managed solely by her husband who is known as *nokma*. Though the husband wields immense power, he has to get the consent of his wife on various issues including sale of property and land. The *chras* of the *nokna* (heiress) can object to any misuse of power. In case of litigation, the *nokna* (heiress) stops coming to the courts of law once formalities have been completed; her *chras* represent her in subsequent appearances.

In the field of administration, women have no part at all. The *nokma* or the village headman, *Laskar* and *Sordar* who administer justice like magistrates in rural areas are all men. Only one Garo woman in a village in Goalpara District has been a member of the village court. To quote Dr. D.N. Majumdar again. 'Women are quite excluded from village administration. A woman can never be a village headman (*nokma*), because a village *nokma* has certain ceremonial functions, and such ceremonial rites cannot be performed by a woman. The position occupied by woman in village affairs is considered to be the lowest and equivalent to that of children. ...In areas where there are bachelors' dormitories, women, excepting the *nokma's* wife, are not allowed to enter the dormitory by the front entrance. In village feasts and ceremonials, women are not allowed to occupy positions reserved for persons of honour. ... In village feasts and ceremonials women do not play any major role. They can be seen busy all the time cooking for guests, fetching water for preparing rice-beer, while the male folk sit and gossip with fellow villagers for days together.'[3]

Women cannot take active part in any religious ceremonies and the priest (*kamal*) is always a male. Though most of the bards are males, women too sing traditional songs and it is mostly women who sing dirges. In ceremonies such as the final burial of the bones of the dead, women take an important part.

In traditional life the workload on the women is heavier than men. True, menfolk fell trees for *jhum*, build houses, make bamboo and cane baskets and other articles for domestic use, yet they have much more leisure time than women.

A woman's day begins at dawn. She cooks for her family, fetches water, washes utensils, nurses the young ones, husks paddy. Before sunrise she serves rice and curry to all members of the family and keeps some wrapped in banana leaves for lunch. Early in the morning she leaves for the *jhum* field and works there side by side with her husband. Often a woman carries her new-born baby in a sling on her back and works in the sun and rain. Usually an expectant mother leaves the field only when the labour pains start. While leaving for home in the evening, a woman does not come empty-handed. She collects and carries firewood, banana leaves, vegetables and crabs and prawns from streams. At night she husks paddy, spins thread out of cotton or removes seeds from cotton during the winter months.

Burdened as she is with bearing and raising children, she is also responsible for keeping the house and the surroundings clean, for looking after domestic animals, for preparation of rice beer etc. She carries heavy loads of *jhum* products to market walking many a kilometres, often carrying her baby in a sling, sells the articles and returns home carrying the purchases. In most villages there are women who are self-supporting, and those who support their husbands (this does not include the disabled) and the whole family. In the traditional life, there is hardly any physical work which is not done by women. Women also help in clearing jungles for *jhum*, collecting and carrying articles for constructing houses.

These services of the woman to her community, her strength and tenacity, her talents and abilities go unrecognized. Often ridicules are hurled on them, a common one being: *Domok wagam gri, michik gisik gri*, meaning just as a goat is without teeth, so a woman lacks brains. There has been no research to assess the psychological damage caused to women by such derogatory remarks. Doubtless, these insults did no good to a woman's self-respect and self-esteem.

Several factors may be ascribed for such a complete subjection of females. Women have far less opportunities than men to go outside their homes and villages to be in contact with the outside world and to widen their experiences as they are tied down by domestic duties.

Their constant engagement in work which is of back-breaking nature does not allow them to stand, watch and observe. There are no avenues open for self-improvement and broadening of knowledge in any field. Women's activities are highly circumscribed by traditional way of life which centres around marriage and *jhum* cultivation. The sole purpose of a woman's existence is marriage, begetting and raising children, and satisfying the desires of men. As for aims, there are none.

Jonmoni D. Shira, writing in 1940, mirrors the absolute and irrefutable truth about the plight of the Garo womenfolk with the sensibilities of an educated woman in the poem *I, The Woman* :

I, THE WOMAN

I have been born a woman
To bear all kinds of difficulties,
Though I lament my misfortune
I cannot alter it.

Poor Eve commited sin
Before the world;
Bringing heavier burdens and worries
Upon the woman.

From birth, her strength is less
Her face is lovelier,
But I am taught
To be under male domination.

From tender age
I have to live under the control of man,
At the slap of my younger brother
I weep loudly.

I cannot act as I please,
There's not a day of happiness for me
I cannot dream of
Even proposing to travel.

I know and understand
The truth,
The bad and the good, the consequences
And the subject matter.

Yet I cannot
So much as open my mouth
Due to the words,
'Silence, you stupid woman!'

To sit in the dumping place of chaff,
To eat the leftovers, is my lot;
I get ridicule from my fellow human beings
Because of my lowliness.

Though I fall in love
With an eligible young man,
I have been forcibly made to give my consent
To one whom I dislike.

When I fall in love with young man
I get into trouble,
For a trifling error
They jilt me.

O Young Man, beware,
Deeds do not simply vanish,
Some time, you too,
May fall into a night of sorrow.

Now I am a married woman,
My difficulties have multiplied;
It is now my duty
To suffer agony in bearing children.

For a slight mistake
I am slapped;
The crying child
Keeps me awake at night.

My husband knows not
My hardship and pains,
I succumb
To more diseases.

In the small hours of the morning
I get up and cook,
I spend the whole day
In the field.

I return home carrying a heavy load
And then I work at home.
Though it is very late at night I cannot rest,
For I have to husk rice.

Out of exhaustion my body becomes thin,
I am no more attractive,
It occurs to my husband
To look for someone else.

Nevertheless, my mind
Has pure thoughts,
Though my husband does me wrong
I bear it patiently.

Souls do not keep silent,
You shall nor remain superior,
As a reward for your deeds
You will not escape from hell.

You, man, therefore,
Beware,
You must surely look into
The grievances of the women.

If my word is wrong,
Refute it,
If you yourself are at fault
Repent now.[4]

Influence of Christianity and Education

From these impediments to their development Christianity and education rescued and uplifted the Garo women to some extent. The efforts of David Scott to bring a lasting solution to the raids committed by Garos in the British Territories finally bore fruit in the establishment of a Christian Mission in 1867 specially designated for the Garos, which established schools while spreading religion.

Christian churches left untouched those social customs which did not clash with christian tenets. Polygyny and *dokchapa* became illegal for christians, but the law of *akim* still held good in so far as a successor had to be provided to a widow or a widower. This custom still continued to plague the Garos, specially women, till the recent period in both urban and rural areas. As has been pointed out, acquisition of high education by women had undermined the power of the *chras* and forcible marriages are becoming rare. In some *mahari* meetings, women's opinions are sought for; they are entrusted with almost equal responsibilities as men.

In the Christian Church discriminations on the ground of sex are practised. Through unwritten rules women have been barred from ascending the pulpit, specially in the urban areas and in conventions. In Tura, two highly educated young men have been fighting, since 1960's, for women's right to speak on the pulpit. Despite opposition from certain quarters, 1980's have seen women speaking the regular church services as well as in Garo Baptist Convention held once every year. Some offices of the church are also entrusted to women. Ordination of women is a subject which has been discussed and debated in the

Baptist churches of north-east India and in the local Baptist Church. However, no ordination of a Garo woman has taken place.

Up to the 1940's the attitude of the illiterate Garos towards education was unfavourable. Girls as well as boys going out of their villages for education were taunted as aping the *roris* (non-garos). Women attending schools preferred to give up their scanty traditional dress and adopted the attire of the non-garo women of the plains. Some literate women learnt the art of weaving on frames and on handloom from their non-garo neighbours of the plains and produced larger clothes called *dakmanda* for women. Since 1930's these clothes have become popular. In making these clothes women have displayed skill and inventiveness while preserving traditional designs. *Dakmanda* making is still a cottage industry among the Garos today.

Traditionally girls were not favoured at the expense of boys; both male and female children were equally welcome into the family. When it came to education, parents discriminated and more importance was laid on the education of sons. Though parents willingly allowed their daughters to attend local school, on completion of the course they did not allow them to continue their studies outside and they were married off. The reason offered for this discriminatory action was that whether educated or not girls would have to stay at home.

The attitude of men towards the education of girls was casual; they never expected them to do well in studies. The low estimate of women in the traditional society continued. This was summed up in the oft-repeated remark by men that girls attend schools to capture men who had jobs with regular income. Some parents were clearly partial to their sons; they took their education seriously and spent more money on them. The prevailing opinion was that girls did not need much education; if their daughters knew how to cook and look after children it was considered quite sufficient. This Victorian attitude seems to have ruled for some time, because many women born in the first decades of the present century depended on their husbands for support though they themselves had some education.

The same prejudice against women finds expression in the male attitude which was held till recently that women should not reach the top even in higher studies. Garo males felt threatened by girls securing higher degrees and would never marry such girls. They wanted to retain their feeling of supremacy and feared that they would lose their prestige and their control over their wives if the latter were more educated.

However prejudiced the pronouncement is, the fear is justified; for since the late 1960's women with higher education were not less than men with similar degrees. It must be admitted that some imbalance existed between educated males and educated females, which made it rather difficult for women above graduate level to find mates from their own community. When such a girl marries a non-garo, she is blamed and denounced; the causes of taking such a step are not investigated and no attempt at analysing social shortcomings is made.

Nevertheless, the situation is not so bleak for women. Education has brought about a revolution in women's world and their status. Her world broadened to include other lands, people and cultures and her experiences widened to an unprecedented degree. Her success in the intellectual world was bound to be recognized; it also brought her liberation from repression and tyranny. An educated woman has a career and other aims besides marriage. She enjoys a sense of fulfilment in her job. Economic independence, besides liberating her from tyranny, gave her self-esteem. True, a spinster is looked down upon and a woman who has either lost or separated from her husband is not respected. Yet she has found an identity of her own and activities to fill her life.

Thus women have been in a better position than ever before to fight against prejudices, conservatism and double standards. They had dared to wear dresses, both Indian and western, which are not their own, against oppostion. The disapproval came despite the fact that women, unlike men, preserved their traditional dress and by wearing it in and outside their land, kept their ethnic identity. Against sneers and backbiting, they have cut their hair when convenience demanded and when they felt that it was justified.

The Present status of women

In the last two decades women have come to the forefront of their community. They are active participants in socio-economic and political changes. Traditionally women have been bread-winners but now she has firmly established herself as a major source of family income. Today most educated women have jobs. They serve in many fields, from teaching to administration, from daily labour to small business. They are neither ineffective nor redundant; they form a workforce to be reckoned with. In construction of homes, they collect materials, supervise work. Some arrange for cutting of bamboo and timber and go to distant villages collect them. Clubs and organizations run by women have made significant contribution to society.

Women's low self-esteem in the past is evident in the submissive, self-abasing tone in which they used to approach men of their choice. The expression 'to live under the shade (protection) of your love' where a man was compared to a tree, was a common phrase. Today among the educated sections such letters are things of the past. It has been observed that women's self-image has now vastly improved; they do not hesitate to undertake any training in addition to their educational qualifications and take up new responsibilities with confidence wherever they are posted. Women's positive attitude to themselves is also seen in their participation in leadership and decision making at various levels.

All the couples from Tura whom I have interviewed concede that husbands consult their wives on most issues. The opinion of the wives are heeded by some husbands. A working woman does not ask money from her husband; she accepts what is offered. The independence of women is likely to be on the increase in the near future as more young women are opting for higher studies. The attitude of parents towards their sons and daughters appear to be impartial now. Girls as well as boys are treasured and are given equal opportunities. In Tura there are three schools exclusively for girls, while they are admitted in all other schools as well. Yet there are more girls seeking admission than the number of seats available.

Many hurdles are yet to be crossed in the women's advance to social justice. A woman's job is not taken seriously by many husbands. A woman officer is just another ordinary wife at home. When she returns home from work she is expected to do shopping, cook, manage the household, look after children, servants, domestic animals and perform umpteen number of chores. When anything goes wrong in the house, she is blamed. An educated mother takes more share of the burden of educating her children. While most mothers help in schoolwork, fathers, who do the same, are few and far between. Feeding, supervising, clothing, nursing the children while they are sick, are regarded as entirely a mother's duty.

Though a few men whom I have interviewed regard their wives as equal partner, most men dominate over them and expect them to be at their service. Some do not want their wives to eat before they do, though traditionally there is no hard and fast rule in this regard. A husband will not ask his wife just home from work whether she will have a cup of tea, though a wife is expected to do so without fail.

Is there any threat to matriliny? A few Garo fathers have given their clan names to their children. A prominent male citizen, who harbours no feelings of insecurity on this point, has this to say, 'I have not taken my father's surname, what right do I have to impose mine on my children?' The basis for the traditional system of inheritance is that males are strong enough to make their living outside their homes, while the youngest daughter might not receive the care of the parents. There are traditionalists who support this custom. Those who are opposed to it argue that males are indisputably more capable of managing parental property.

Has the Garo woman attained the status envisaged in the Constitution of India? The answer is clearly no. Illiteracy is rampant; ignorance hinders development. The attitude of men towards women's education has not changed. Few men want their wives to have higher qualification and very few offer encouragement to their wives to improve their lot. Crimes against women are on the increase. Rape and abduction have become more widespread than before. Bigamy and polygamy are practised even by christians. Women continue to bear this without a murmur of protest and allow themselves to be trampled upon. On desertion, a woman does not seek divorce and redress. Women labourers are paid less. At present only one woman M.L.A. represents the Garo women.

Strategy for development

For overall development and integration of women into building their society and the country, education among them should be made universal and illiteracy should be wiped out. According to 1981 census the female literacy in West Garo Hills is 19.55% and 27.66% in East Garo Hills. Ignorance is the bane of women specially in the rural areas. In addition to formal education, women should be enlightened about various social ills and be given vocational education. It has been observed that an educated woman uplifts the whole family. Napoleon had said, 'The future destiny of the child is always the work of the mother.' An awareness should be created among the women about social abuses; repressive custom should be removed. Confidence and awareness of women's potential for development as also a knowledge of their rights and privileges must be imparted to them. A planned approach should be formulated for the overall development of women to enable them to realise their full potentials and to participate fully in the socio-cultural, political and economic development of the country.

REFERENCES

1. Majumdar, D.N., *The Tribes of North-East India*, pp. 307-8.
2. Majumdar, D.N. and Goswami, M.C., *Social Institutions of the Garo of Meghalaya*, pp. 59-60.
3. *Ibid*, pp. 60-61.
4. Translated from the Garo by the present Author.

7

REPORT

Abhijit Choudhury

The Centre for Literary and Cultural Studies, North-Eastern Hill University, Shillong, organised a Seminar on the *Status of Women in Tribal Cultures of Meghalaya* on 13-14 July, 1988, in collaboration with Indian Council of Social Science Research, North-Eastern Regional Centre, Shillong, at the Seminar Hall of the Mayurbhanj Campus of NEHU.

The Seminar was inaugurated by Prof. R.K. Mishra, Vice-Chancellor, NEHU, on July 13. Prof. J.B. Bhattacharjee, Dean, School of Social Sciences, NEHU, presided over the inaugural session. Mr. P. Jhingan gave the vote of thanks.

Welcoming the participants to the inaugural session, Dr. Soumen Sen, Head, Centre for Literary and Cultural Studies and Director of the Seminar, emphasized that people are not much aware of the very important role women play in society. In the historical societies inequality in rights and positions between men and women has been one of the most glaring inconsistencies, he said. In the tribal societies of the north-eastern region, however, a somewhat different picture is discerned. But here also the status and role of women are changing in an emerging situation. Referring to the practice of matriliny in the

Khasi-Jaintia, and Garo societies in Meghalaya, Dr. Sen posed a few questions : Does matriliny mean that women have been assigned a greater role in social life? If so, what is that role and if not, what role has actually been assigned to them? Has there been any change in their status over the years?

Inaugurating the Seminar, the Vice-Chancellor, Dr. R.K. Mishra dwelt at length on the women's place and role in society. He believed that women basically needed shelter and care. He said his was the stand point of a philosopher. Prof. J.B. Bhattacharjee, Dean of the School of Social Sciences, stressed the importance of such studies which might help our understanding of the status and role of women under matriliny in the Khasi, Jaintia and Garo societies of Meghalaya in both traditional and emerging situations.

The first academic session followed the inauguration with Prof. I.M. Simon, of the Khasi Department of NEHU and Prof. P.K. Mishra, Head of the Anthropology Department as the chair person at initial and later stages of deliberations respectively. This session was devoted to the Khasi scene. Prof. Juanita War of the Department of Linguistics, NEHU, and Ms. I.M. Syiem, Department of Sociology, St. Edmund's College, Shillong, presented their papers 'Status of Women in Traditional Khasi Culture' and 'Women in Khasi Society'. Both the papers discussed the role of Khasi women in traditional social, economic and political systems and then traced the changes taking place in contemporary situation. Opening her deliberations, Prof. War challenged the notion that women would always like to be cared. In a similar tone, Ms. Syiem declared that women did not need to prove that they were women. There was no necessity, indeed, of comparisons with men since women's responses to their environs were different from those of men.

Prof. War asserted that men and women must play a complementary role in order to sustain the society. She argued that while the status and role assigned to men and women vary from society to society due to religion, types of social and family organizations and social customs, etc., the in-built mechanisms of maintaining social equality between men and women in tribal societies have remained more or less intact. In the traditional Khasi systems and under the present circumstances, both the paper-writers pointed out, Khasi women have been and are treated as the symbol of purity and goodness. Both Prof. War and Ms. Syiem cited that the *Khadduh* (the youngest daughter) as the keeper of religion (*Ka bat ia ka niam*), held a sacred position in her home. Her home is the place of worship (*Ka Iing Niam*). Women are not merely a factor of continuity of the clan (*Kur*), but they sustain it too. This fact is reflected in the special place accorded to the Khasi mother in family and society. Clan lineage is stressed through the *Ka Iawbei* (ancestress) who is highly revered. However, women are not merely the keeper of house and family. They are the custodian of social relationships as well. Because, the maintenance of Khasi matriliny - based on inheritance of property along the matrilineage – is intricately balanced on *kinship* structure. This point was brought home by both the writers. The *Khadduh* (the youngest daughter) is the custodian of family property and, therefore, accountable to the *Durbar* of uncles and brothers. Any family member and kinsman, passing through rainy days, has to be taken care of by her. In her role as *ka bat ia ka niam*, the *Khadduh* is a kind of priestess assisting her maternal uncle in the rites.

The Khasi women have always played important role in socio-economic life. The *Khadduh*, for instance, is the custodian of family property which is 'more of a joint family trust' (Ms. Syiem). However, the *Khadduh* is not the heiress to ancestral property as it is simply transmitted to the next generations through her. Both Dr. War and Ms. Syiem observed that the *Khadduh* used to be the custodian of honour of her *Kur* from the point of view of her social obligations which she inherited by virtue of her unique status in Khasi socio-cultural and economic life.

Both the writers stressed that the customary sanctions regarding marriage were strictly followed. In the Khasi matrilineal system sexual assaults and adultery (*Ka Klim*) are considered sacriligeous. It has always been the duty and responsibility of the men to protect the honour and dignity of women. Marriage is a sacred affair. The Khasi society is characterized by free mixing of the two sexes. However, it cannot be called a 'permissive' society in the modern sense of the term, as moral sanctions and injunctions regulate their interactions.

Although women participated very actively in the socio-cultural and economic life of the Khasis they were not allowed to participate in political and administrative affairs in general. Of course, there have been some exceptions including that of the position of priestess in the Syiem's household (*Syiemsad*), and of *Ka Lar*, the female Syiem of the Nobosohphoh Syiemship. This point is particularly interesting from the angles of (i) its historical background traced to some extent by Dr. War, and (ii) modern changes analysed by both the writers. Historically, women treated politics as men's work (*Ka Kam Ki Rangbah*). Even in modern times, barring a few exceptions, women generally tend to remain away from active politics.

Tracing the emerging trends today, the writers observed that factors of education, christian missionary activities, necessity to join public services to augment family income, and modern entrepreneurial endeavours, etc., are effecting the status of women to some extent in the sense that new equations in social relationships and interactions are appearing. Professional life has got its own limitations and problems. Even the kinship functions are effected. For instance, in traditional Khasi system, the

Ki Kha (paternal relatives) were recognised as *ki nongai ki nongsei rynieng* (the givers of life and stature) and hence were loved and respected. *U Thawlang* (the father-progenitor) was respected as much as *Ka Meikha*. At the same time, the maternal male-kins were looked upon as *Ki nongbtin lynti, Ki nongduai phirat bad Ki nongsaid nongthew* (the guardians, the communicators, the diviners and the pleaders) who maintained the intricate system of matriliny. The maternal uncles had a dual role in traditional society as (i) maternal uncles in the *Kur*, and (ii) fathers in their households. Today, however, this second role is taking over the first. The mechanical way of life in modern society, busy daily schedules and other problems are some of the factors which now restrict their role as maternal uncles to the *Kur*. Both the writers mentioned that dominated by its patriarchal values, the Church is yet to offer the position of say, the pastor, to women in Khasi Hills. Increasingly as some researches reveal, though the Khasi women are increasingly becoming forward looking, they are not essentially aggressive in their social attitude inspite of the new trends emerging in a society in transition.

Opening the session to discussions, Prof. P.K. Mishra observed that these papers were complementary to each other. Moreover, what was more significant was that these papers represented the *insiders*' viewpoints on the question of women's status in tribal cultures. Mr. J.N. Choudhury believed that the theme of the Seminar should not have been qualified by an adjective like 'Tribal' as even in the Indian constitution this term is not used and it still awaits a definition. He cited from historical evidence, of the Khasis having their own political systems. It was implicit, perhaps, in his comments that when the institution of Kingship/State is formed in a community then it ceases to remain at the stage of 'tribe'/tribal formation'. However, considering it a broader issue Dr. Mishra postponed discussion on this point.

Dr. Chitralekha Verma commented that it could not be said that men and women were equal from biological point of view. According to her, in the modern world the gadgets as time-saving elements provide more spare time to women. It is a question as to how they use it. She asked if there really was any scope for regarding women as *individuals* or as *occupants of status and role* in a particular society. She wanted to know if there was any data that women were regarded as *individuals* in the Khasi society. She also felt that as an anthropologist, she did not find the term 'maternal descendants' a precise one. Her observation was that the term 'adultery' was related to women only in the *dictionary* sense of the term. She asked whether there was any punishment in the Khasi society for a man committing adultery. Mrs. Verma expressed her doubt if there was any scientific foundation of thinking that the attitude of women and their world view were different from men. Ms. Syiem reacted that (i) there was no doubt about biological differences. However, emotions are *conditioned* by various factors; (ii) Roles are probably based on the *sexual axis*; (iii) Talking about men and women in terms of using the gadgets there is not much difference at the intellectual level; and (iv) There is a correlation between the *roles* and *actions* of the individuals. Roles are *occupied* by human beings. Therefore, there cannot be any *rigidity* about it. Though *roles* may come first, *personality* factor cannot be ignored as it creates new patterns in social relationship.

Ms. Syiem felt that *personality* and *role* are *same* for men and women. Education, of course, may lead the women to ask about themselves and their traditional roles. In reply to Mrs. Verma, she said that by 'matrilineal descendants' she meant *matrilineal kinship group*. However, Prof. A.C. Bhagawati interjected that in anthropological parlance it should mean 'matrilineal descent group'. Attending to the interaction between Mrs. Verma and Ms. Syiem, one may recall the observations made by Desmond Morris, a reductionist philosopher of Science, about the biological basis of human behaviour and of the basic differences between men and women.

Principal S.K. Acharya felt that these two papers reflected the standpoints of urban, educated middle class Khasis. Prof. P.K. Mishra, later in his views from the chair, agreed to this observation and added that perhaps these views might not exactly fit in the situation in the case of *rural* Khasi women. Acharya observed that only a comparison with the situation in African tribes might help one in a proper appreciation as to what extent the Khasi women enjoy higher social status. He cited the case of the Ashanti tribe in Africa, among whom the womenfolk can do without menfold. He found that the question of gross inequalities between men and women in the Khasi society have not been depicted in the papers.

The two writers, Dr, War and Ms. Syiem, took up the question of adultery. *Polygamy* is allowed only in exigencies like say, barrenness of the first wife. In the event of taking a second woman, otherwise, a man can not have her from the same village and he is required to pay some money which is equivalent to somekind of punishment. Khasi males are allowed to have a second wife but she cannot enjoy the same status with his *first* wife. Ms. Syiem objected to Acharya's comment that women might have been treated in isolation in these papers as she felt that men and women cannot be treated in isolation. Dr. War said that in urban areas women do more work. However, it depends on the families. According to her, *Kinship* is more important than the territorial dimension. Dr. War and Ms. Syiem were outright in agreeing that theirs' were essentially 'urban middle class' viewpoints. At this juncture Prof. P.K. Mishra sought to induce reactions from the Khasi gentlemen present in the house. Mr. Henry Lamin commented that in the present day context the position of the Khasi menfolk is gradually deteriorating. However, as it appears the Khasi youth, especially the males, are avoiding their duties and responsibilities. Objecting to the term 'equal status,' he added elements of humour when he said that this seminar should have been given as its theme, 'The Status of Men in Tribal Cultures of Meghalaya'. Dr. K.M. Warjri observed that the practices today are different from what these used to be. Khasi women do not participate in elections say, under the new political system since they have got overwhelming involvement in activities in other spheres of life. They have got to select their priorities. Heavy work load is given to them by the culture in which they grow up. However, in the fields of education and civil services women clearly dominate. Mrs. Rina Lyngdoh observed that these points were overlooked in these papers.

Putting her observations, Dr. Mrs. Biloris Lyndem cited her experience to show that at the *durbar* level menfolk never allowed the women to have a say in public life, except a few exceptions. Dr. P. Nayak observed that contrary to the situation elsewhere in India, in Meghalaya political alienation of particularly the rural women did not seem to appear, as *tradition* backed them in a show of roles. It is reversed here in the political alienation of menfolk. According to him, inequalities are coming up now, affecting women's status in the same way as it does in the rest of the country. Khasi women are cushioned off from political role by a mere show of respect for their traditional status which can be correlated that in the global context wherein women are set apart from active political roles by fetishizing their roles as pure, etc. Dr. War agreed with Dr. Nayak that probably tradition backed the women in a show of roles. However, she declined to give comment on reversal of alienation on menfolk here, as she admitted she did not give thought to this aspect. She agreed with Nayak that women liked to be content with their traditional privileges. It was agreed that the rise of nuclear families, etc., are going to redefine the traditional role of women. However, areas of changes can be studied in supplementary works. Dr. K. Bhatt pointed out that roles were well-defined in traditional systems and not in modern ones. To understand the process of transformation from tradition to modernity, one requires to find out the *linkages* between traditional and modern societies. In reply to Prof. A.C. Bhagawati's question if women take up any role in the Church in the West, Ms. Syiem pointed out that Western women are appointed as pastors in mainly the Presbyterian Church. Clarifying her position on the changing role of the maternal uncles and the *Khadduh* in present day society, she said that roles are not as exactly defined in modern society as it used to be in traditional societies.

Dr. P.M. Passah felt that the two papers lead to *implicit* conclusion that the Khasi society is a female-dominated society. Consequently, the status of Khasi women cannot be lower but higher, if not equal, to that of Khasi men. He observed that from this stand-point it is immaterial whether the Khasi women participated or not in active politics. Drawing attention to earlier discussion on 'personality' factor, Prof. M.N. Karna observed that this point needed serious discussion. Basic personality types are factors that cannot be ignored. *Personality* operates in a larger value frame. There cannot be any *free* personality in any society. Addressing from the chair, Dr. P.K. Mishra, among other points, hazarded a hypothesis that whatever the role of the *khadduh*-either as 'custodian' or'inheritor' of property those without any direct share in property may be compelled or motivated to seek new openings through entrepreneurship. This motivation of the *non-khaddus* needs study. Mentioning that the Khasi society is one of the very few matrilineal societies of the world, he cited his experiences of working among two classical food gathering communities. One of them, living in caves in Kerala, have the males dominating over the women; whereas among the Jarwas of Andaman, women dominate absolutely without any ambiguity. Therefore, there cannot be any correlation between the economic system and the status of particualr sex.

After this session of thoroughly provocatives points and counter-points, the second academic session began with Dr. Mrs. Biloris Lyndem of the Centre for Adult and Continuing Education, NEHU, as the Chairperson. Its theme was the *Garo Situation*. Dr. Mrs. Caroline R. Marak of Tura Government College presented the only paper of this session. The title of her paper was 'Status of Women in Garo Culture'. She started with the Garo myths to show the high honour bestowed on the womenfolk. Tracing the Garo matriliny in its traditional form, wherein the Garo womenfolk had a predominant socio-cultural and economic role to play, Mrs. Marak observed that in 'actual' situations they were not treated as they deserved. She cited the *Law of Akim*, an arrangement of remarriage of the widows or the widowers - as the case may be – to show that women are often subjected to coercion in this context. However, various factors, including especially Christianity and missionary educational endeavours, have played to change the world view and attitude of the Garo womenfolk, she said. Women have always been denied the position of *Nokma* (Village Headmanship) and also direct and active participation in religious ceremonies. There was only one exception where a Garo woman in a village in Goalpara District (Assam) has been a member of village court. The husband has the final word in 'exercising authority' over property. Even the husband of the *nokna* (heiress) manages land on her behalf. He is also known as the *nokma*. However, her consent is needed in dealing with the property. The *chras* (male relatives) of Garo women maintain control over them (the womenfolk). Mrs. Marak cited several factors, including circumscription of women's lives by traditional way veering round marriage and *jhum* cultivation, which are responsible for complete subjugation of Garo women. Although in the last two decades women have come to the forefront of their community, yet many males have reservations about their rights. Most men try to dominate over women inspite of the latter taking a lion's share of the burden of family lores and works. Mrs. Marak cited many factors responsible for the womenfolk not attaining the status envisaged for women in the Indian Constitution. She suggested, among others, adequate educational facilities for women to raise the level of their self-confidence and awareness of their own potentials. They must be aware of their rights and privileges of they are to contribute towards social development.

Opening this paper to discussion, Dr. Lyndem considered it a very interesting assessment of the 'actual' situation in the traditional Garo society. Meanings are implied as Mrs. Marak refrained from giving any analysis of particularly the Garo myths. Principal S.K. Acharya wanted to know if there was any difference in the inheritance pattern between Garo and Khasi societies. It has to be looked into whether the system of inheritance leads to the low status of Garo women. He felt that comparison of this system in Khasi and Garo societies may help one to understand the current situation. He asked if one can evolve some system that might improve the situation. But Prof. A.C. Bhagawati said that such a stand would be too hypothetical. Mr. P.R. Mawthoh disagreed with Principal Acharya's view that one may discard explanation on the basis of conversion to Christianity to see the current situation of transition. Dr. Juanita War and Principal Acharya discussed the question of relationship between *inheritance* and *status pattern*. Prof. Bhagawati commented that 'may be the need of looking after the aged/ageing couples influences the Garo system of inheritance of property. Mrs. Marak replied that traditionally, some properties go to the male members too. Prof. M.N. Karna observed that the whole question of *patriliny* vs *matriliny* could be a subject of debate. He pointed out that Mrs. Marak's paper was a clear testimony that women may not essentially enjoy high status due to matriliny. He brought analogies from situations in patriliny among central Indian tribes. Identifying three levels of the Garo society namely, (i) *traditional*, (ii) *recent* and (iii) Christianized, Prof. Karna submitted that in *ideal* typical situation there might not have been lower status of women in traditional system. It must have been a later phenomenon. He also expressed his doubt as to whether any religion for that matter can provide an inherent mechanism to accord a higher status to a segment in a given society through conversion. For instance, it is doubtful if the Hindus gained in status by converting to either Islam or Christianity. Historically, the Hindu *caste* system also prevails among such converts. He stressed the need of discussion of the situation wherein a matrilineal society say, in north-eastern India, is implanted in a patrilineal world view provided by Christianity. There must be some commitment if one is so articulate about the status of women today, he said and added that it is to be seriously taken up. At this point, Prof. Bhagawati added that the observations of Mrs. Marak cut through a universe covering the patrilineal as well as matrilineal societies. According to him, her observations are equally applicable to the Assamese society. However, she has dealt with an educated segment of the society, to whom patriliny and matriliny may not be relevant at all. He agreed with Prof. Karna that lower status was not a phenomenon in ideal traditional system. Something was wrong, according to Prof. Bhagawati, to think that women were looked upon as sex object considering the overall socio-cultural and economic role played by the Garo women. Taking up the two aspects of this paper, viz., (i) traditional structure and (ii) modern developments, he pointed to the interwined relationship between the role of Christianity and coming of education (i.e., going to church meant going to school) influencing the outlook and attitude of the Garo women.

Mrs. Marak replied that virtually no material are available for the pre-British days on these questions of status in traditional Garo society. No Garo scholar has done any work so far. She tried to contact some elderly

Garos but unfortunately many of them had already died. Therefore, she failed to trace the origin of the Garo matriliny. Mr. P.R. Mawthoh observed that conversion to Christianity did not put any bar on social interaction in the traditional system. Dr. J. War observed that women in patrilineal Naga and Mizo societies enjoy good status. According to her, Christianity provides a mechanism of complementary relationship based on mutual respect between the two sexes. Prof. Bhagawati felt that this must have been more so with the Garo society. Talking about the Christian Garos Mrs. Marak pointed out that with the advent of Christianity the world view had changed and knowledge was widened. While the menfolk discarded say, their traditional attires for western dresses the womenfolk did not do so. The changed attitude of the menfolk, in this case, might have sprang from their consciousness about their scanty dress. In reply to Mr. Henry Lamin's observation on the lack of any say in matters of decision making on the part of the Garo womenfolk, Mrs. Marak said that only men folk decided the issues. Interacting with Mrs. Marak, Mr. P.R. Mawthoh, Principal Acharya and Prof. Bhagawati on the role of Christianity, Prof. Karna pointed out that there should not be any confusion between mythology, theology and social organization. The question is how a given religious system is articulated. Theoretically speaking, religion is a *personal domain* of man. But such premises cannot be accepted, he said. So, social organization must be taken into account. Here, he disagreed with Mr. Mawthoh. Christianity helped the spread of literacy say, in Mizoram. But, he asked, if it really helped the spread of *education* in the north-eastern region as a whole. In India, however, Christianity has raised the standard of life and status for the tribals. But Christianity should not be overemphasized in the analysis of developmental problems he added. Smti Elizabeth Warjri observed that Christianity came with the Biblical concept of patrilineal society. As a result of this influence, women are never given any high position in the Church. According to her, in the War area of Khasi Hills there exists equal share of property between men and women. Generally speaking, the Khasi women have more share of property which constitutes an economic source of status for women.

At this stage, Smti Biana Momin from Tura Government College, joined discussion to obsesrve that (i) in traditional Garo Society girls were not allowed to school. Only after the advent of Christianity did this attitude change. Therefore, the situation might have been different from those in the other tribal areas of the north-eastern region; (ii) in traditional society, too, the status of women was low. But now it has changed with the coming of education etc. Prof. Karna agreed with this point and said that education by itself cannot give status to women in society. It is only a means of improving their status. Mr. Aniruddha Burman wanted a clarification whether one can say that Garo Society is *patriarchal* with *matriliny in inheritance pattern*. Mr. Henry Lamin thought that from this paper it appearaed that the Garo social system was patriarchal with matrilineage.

Dr. P. Nayak's observation that missionary education developed sectarian attitude among a section of women, led to a debate on the identity of Christianity and education and their role in the status of women. Once again Principal Acharya, Mr. P.R. Mawthoh, Ms. I.M. Syiem, Dr. Chitralekha Verma and others joined the issue. Dr. Lyndem said that as for the Khasi society, the missionaries originally did not have any say on traditional pattern/system. Ms. Syiem felt that the role of Khasi women were affected by Christian patriarchal value system, especially among the converts. Same is true of any other religious systems like say, Islam. On the relation between eduction and Christianity, Ms. Syiem pointed out that mere raising of status could not solve women's problems. Women's role in society was not seriously thought about. Prof. Karna intervened to say that he wanted to know exactly this point. Accordingly to him, mere raising of status was not enough. He asked: what about their changing roles in view of new developments? He added that mere higher education could not bring about higher education in the sense of societal developments. He could not accept Mr. Mawthoh's stand that Christianity and missionary education played a very special role. He observed that new linkages established by the processes operating outside the traditional system are important in the study of the problems of the north-east. The colonial rulers used say, the institution of syiemship, to enter the system.

Dr. Verma said that Christianity did not really make the people familiar with/aware of their own cultures/country rather than more with Europe. However, she joined issues with Dr. Nayak on the latter's comment that the dominant bias of this paper was to look at menfolk as the villain for all the women's sufferings. Of course, Mrs. Marak already pointed out that she actually emphasized women's 'ignorance' of their own positions and problems rather than men's villainy.

Dr. K.M. Wavjri observed that the Muslim Khasis do not follow matriliny as such. Evidently, the status of Khasi women in such segments is low. He drew comparisons with the Nayyars of Kerala.

The third academic session addressed itself to the Jaintia situation. With Prof. B. Pakem, Hony. Director, North-eastern Regional Centre of ICSSR, in Chair; two scholars presented their papers. Dr. P.M. Passah of the Department of Economics, NEHU, and Dr. L.S. Gassah of the Political Science Department, NEHU, had identical titles for their papers which read: 'Status of Women in Jaintia Culture'. Both the authors traced the traditional pattern of Jaintia matriliny and its socio-cultural, economic as well as political roles of women. Jaintia matriliny is *more or less* identical with that of the Khasis. Like in the Khasi polity, the Jaintia polity, including its system of election to traditional chiefships etc., did not encourage women's participation as such. Jaintia women normally treated politics as the domain of menfolk. However, as in the Khasi system, there have been exceptions.

The role and significance of *Ka Khadduh* was highlighted in these papers as was the case with those on Khasi system. In view of the problems of *inheritance of property*, its significance can be understood. However, women's role is that of a *custodian* only. The matriliny normally used to play a dominant role. But now-a-days, due to various factors, including the modern day living, the father's role in family is becoming increasingly apparent. The factors of modernization such as administrative machinery, competitive enterprise in economy, women's participation in employment and business avenues, transport and communication, Christianity and education have played and are playing their due roles in the current phase of *transition* of the Khasi-Jaintia societies affecting all aspects of their lives. *Matriliny* is naturally experiencing new problems.

According to Dr. Passah, as in the Khasi society, the foundation of the Jaintia matriliny rested on the honour and dignity of women. From the point of view of family organization and religious life women play significant roles as administrators of household affairs and as priestesses. As in the Khasi society, the husband is normally neutral to his wife's activities from the point of view of tradition. A husband used to be a stranger in his wife's house. But as already cited above, this position is changing now. Dr. Gassah mentioned a number of authors, including Khasi-Jaintia ones, who have contributed to the understanding of the traditional systems. He drew attention to the fact that one school of thought, especially among the Khasi-Jaintia thinkers, pleaded immediate change over from matrilineal to patrilineal system of inheritance, descent and succession. Such debates are characteristic of any transitional society, he said. Among others, he raised two important points:

(i) It is a taboo on Jaintia women to marry a non-tribal or a person from other religious groups. Their children are traditionally debarred from inheritance of family property and privileges in religious ceremonies;

(ii) nobody infact inherits family/ancestral property; they only get a share of it. In this sense, the *Ka Khadduh* is the custodian of this property and keeps/maintains all shares in it together.

He mentioned two kinds of property, namely, *Yongrim* (inalienable) and *Yutran* (alienable). While the former is *ancestral*, the latter is *personal*. The *Ka Khadduh* is the mere custodian of *Yongrim* which is actually managed by her male matrikins. However, one can have acquired personal property or *Yutran* which may be alienated if the owner wanted so. He also discussed the changes currently taking place in the Jaintia society affecting its ethos etc.

The discussions on these papers began with Prof. A.C. Bhagawati citing the vising status (ie., visiting his wife at night to leave at dawn) of the husband in traditional Jaintia system. He inquired if such husbands had any economic obligations/responsibilities in the bringing up of their children. He drew a close parallel with the Nambudiri Brahmins and the Nayyars of the Malabar Coast where a Nambudiri Brahmin having Nayyar wife has his children/offspring brought up as Nayyars. Dr. Passah replied that traditionally economic obligations did not exist. In the event of family marriages he may send token gifts. However, it is not customary. The Chairperson, Prof. Pakem added that it was found in some traditional villages that when his children were mature enough, a separate household was built for him to stay with his wife. Prof. Bhagawati asked Dr. Passah if there is any obligation on the part of the wife's male matrikins in the emerging urban situation say, at Jowai, where there may be *nuclear families* involving only husband and wife. Prof. Pakem intervened and said that they do have such responsibilities and work for wife's family even if a nuclear family use say, a government quarter as residence.

Dr. Soumen Sen wondered why the society felt the need to create tenets prohibiting women's participation in administration in traditional system. So far as the housefold affairs are concerned women are mere custodians but not decision-makers. It is a striking situation which needs attention. Dr. Gassah reacted that myths and legends reflect women's participation in state affairs. However, there is dearth of material which may throw light on any stage when women might have actively participated in public affairs. Dr. Passah felt that women feel shy to participate. Dr. Sen intervened to say that it must be a modern situation. To this Dr. Passah said that women themselves avoided politics and there must have been some sort of inhibitions. Dr. Gassah agreed with Dr. Passah on this question. Military necessity also debarred women from politics and decision-making process. Only male-franchise was allowed in the traditional system of electing chiefs. However, Prof. Pakem mentioned *Piang Sariang* as a legendary woman ruler. At this stage, Mr. Gabriel wanted to know how one can understand this question from the angle of modern concepts of politics. There was not much discussion on this important question.

Dr. Apurba Baruah pointed out that women were custodians of ancestral property and not its managers. They do not enjoy sufficient role as ruler/decision-makers. Does then, matriliny enhance their position in society in the real sense of the term? What exactly is their role? Dr. Barua considered these questions valid as similar situations are prevalent in patrilineal societies. Prof. Pakem replied that it was difficult to answer. Women were never entirely excluded from political processes. Perhaps topography, distance between the villages, etc., put restrictions on the women's becoming state officials. The state priest must have solicited assistance from the women in ritual ceremonies. Dr. Juanita War tried to explain the reasons of women's non-participation in politics. According to her (i) menfolk were mostly involved in wars and hence had to take strategic decisions; (ii) *Durbars* were usually held in orderly manner. Hence women, youth and drunks were not allowed as they were considered not much useful in decision-making. Prof. Pakem added that menfolk took decisions but women's consent was also sought. It would be wrong to say that women did not altogether participate in the process. He mentioned that in the contiguous patrilineal societies there were influences of the Jaintia matrilineal system. Much importance is attached to women's role in such societies.

Dr. Pakem replied to Dr. Baruah's question on sharing and disposal of ancestral property that no one could sell it unless there was common consent in the event of exigencies. Prof. A.C. Sinha wanted to know what type of property could be disposed of. To this, Dr. Passah replied that they do have disposable properties including household goods and moveable properties, for example, utensils, gold and silver. Land under wet cultivation as well as livestock are disposable. Mrs. Dipali Chatterjee asked about the status of unmarried women. Dr. Gassah replied that there was no special status for an unmarried woman if she was not the youngest daughter. Prof. Pakem added that in traditional society, unmarried women continued to live in the mother's household, with common kitchen. Dr. Biloris Lyndem observed that unmarried women were never looked down upon in Khasi, Jaintia and Garo societies. Mrs. Caroline Marak asked about the attitude of society to such women. Dr. Passah replied that it was one of spirit of co-operation. Prof. Bhagawati thought that in patrilineal societies the question of unmarried women may create problems. But there must be very few unmarried women in the Jaintia society. Mr.

Gabriel said: we are facing a society which does not assign any particular merit to this problem. He agreed with Prof. Bhagawati that such a question could be hypothetical as it reflected two different kinds of attitude. In reply to another question from Mr. A. Choudhury, Dr. Gassah said that people even used to look down upon a traditional Jaintia lady marrying a Christian convert. But changes in attitude are taking place. However, in the case of traditional religious practices the taboos on the offsprings of such marriages are still followed. Mrs. Rina Lyndoh, Dr.K.M. Wavjiri and Principal Acharya participated in this discussion.

Mrs. Caroline Marak asked as to why the Jaintia women felt the need to form a women's wing within the Presbyterian Church. Dr. Passah replied that they wanted it to give expression to their activities. However, Dr. Baruah thought that there might have been reasons not directly linked to a matrilineal system. Prof. Pakem agreed to such probabilities as certain kind of activities, for example, collection of donation are done exclusively by women. Women are denied appointment as pastors in the Church including the Baptist Church. Ms. Syiem raised a point that in some societies women may have more roles in general. What is the attitude of the society? Prof. Bhagawati gave the example of childbearing and the role of women in it to say that certain values are attached to male and female offsprings influencing the pattern of their upbringing. Different patterns of investments for male and female children could be observed, for instance, in education. He asked if in the matrilineal context of Jaintia society in emerging situation one noticed such tendencies. A lady participant, however, differed on the question of differential treatments. She said it might vary from family to family. Mr. Lamin observed that though in the Jaintia society they prefer boys, still they believe that the birth of a female child is a blessing since woman is the *continuator* of the lineage. It is a general tendency from the standpoint of lineage. However, in other matters the attitude may vary from family to family. Dr. Passah observed that no discrimination is practised between a boy and a girl. Dr. Gassah pointed out that in the southern part of the Jaintia Hills the situation was not much different. Continuation of clan/lineage is more important, although in the context of agricultural activities they may prefer to have more boys since they can be of much help. Prof. Pakem added that in the far-eastern side, the patrilineal *Biate* tribe prefer boys to girls.

Dr. A. Baruah referred to the general complaint of women in the Khasi-Jaintia hills about irresponsible attitude of menfolk which creates a difficult situation. He asked if in the context of change it did not mean a low status for women in practice. A lady participant said that boys given more education to probably avert this kind of situation in the context of change. Dr. Gassah admitted that it was a problem. But concrete answer to Dr. Baruah's question may not be possible as it is a debateble point. Dr. Passah opined, it may not be a general feature with the Jaintias. Dr. War thought that *early dating* might be one of the factors why the boys tend to shirk responsibilities. Prof. Pakem concluded this session with his observation that statistics as indicators may not be reliable all the time. Changes are taking place, and one has to accept that the main question in urban as well as rural areas is: how to adjust the relationship and status of men and women.

Four major emphases emerged from the discussion during the third Session. These were:

(i) Confusions as to whether the Jaintia society represented a matrilineal system with elements of patriliny;

(ii) Contradictions in the status of women in familial and socio-political sectors;

(iii) Certain nuances regarding the attitude to women

were subtle indicating the exact trends which required to be traced; and

(iv) In the modern context, the workloads on women as well as their responsibilities have tremendously increased.

The Valedictory Session was presided over by Prof. A.C. Bhagawati of the Department of Anthropology, Gauhati University. The report prepared by Mr.Abhijit Choudhury of the Department of History, St. Edmund's College, who was the Chief Rapporteur and assisted by Mr. Kishore Bhattacharjee, U.G.C. research fellow in Anthropology in Gauhati University, was presented. Discussions on this report was followed by Prof. Bhagawati's invitation to the participants to arrive at some understanding of the *nature* and *problems* of *matriliny*, as the tribal societies of Meghalaya presented unique phenomena. Prof. Bhagawati delineated *three* broad areas for consideration in terms of (i) opportunities and discriminations thereof vis-a-vis women, (ii) Women's position in power structure, and (iii) definition of the role of a particular sex from ideological point of view. These, he felt, might help one in understanding the problems of *position* and *status* of women. It led to debate, for instance, on the questions of quantificatory and qualitative comparisons with reference to the problem of scientific enquiry. Prof. P.K. Mishra said that Prof. Bhagawati had raised a pertinent question as to *what should be the measure of status* of say, women (Prof. Bhagawati cited E. E. Evans-Pritchard's stand in this context of scientific enquiry). But Prof. Mishra felt, it was difficult to determine status through fixed parametres because ranking of these parametres are dissimilar according to cultures. He proposed that until *real* units of quantification were identified, one could not establish scientific enquiry. At this point, Mr. Kishore Bhattacharjee observed that qualitative comparisons could also be regarded as scientific. According to him, anthropological comparisons are primarily qualitative. Prof. A. C. Sinha felt that the *transitional* cultures presented a complex situation where changing roles develop a new matrix of status. Prof. Bhagawati cited Prof. Mishra's hypothesis (which the latter hazarded during the first business session) to say that change in roles was related to traditional social structure which affected the postion of individuals. In the case of say, the Khasi society, the non-inheriting sisters take to entrepreneurship.

Principal S.K. Acharya, Prof. P.K. Mishra, Prof. A.P. Sinha, Dr. P. Nayak, Dr. A. Baruah, Dr. B. Dutta Ray and Mr. Butola participated in the debates on many issues that emerged during these discussions. Mr. P.R. Mawthoh, Ms. I.M. Syiem, Dr. L.S. Gassah and Ms. Jaya Choudhury also took part. Principal Acharya felt that there have been worst type of male domination not only in the Garo society but also in the Khasi society. Mr. P.R. Mawthoh was critical of such a stand and said that considering the realities of social situation in Meghalaya's tribal milieu., here it could be *men's lib.* movement unlike the other societies elsewhere. Prof. Mishra believed that there was nothing, intrinsically, like high or low status. Even the insiders could have different perspectives. But Dr. Baruah was critical about Prof. Mishra's stand saying that opinions are conditioned by society. Moreover, agencies of socialization are in the hands of men including educational institutions, church, etc. Participating in this debate, Dr. Nayak talked about the three levels of issues, viz.*economic opportunities*, *political power* and *ideological struggle* which he considered as important parametres. But Prof. Mishra asked as to how one could judge a society. He went on to ask, how universal values could be fitted into say, the Khasi matrilineal system. He wanted the universal values be objectively assessed and felt that the social scientists go through socialization themselves. According to him both Nayak and Baruah were wrong in their positions. Raising questions on the functional roles of the tribal women, Dr. Dutta Ray observed that the media including T.V. and cinema have influenced the thinking process of the tribal women. He agreed that women in the Khasi-Pnar societies were mere *custodians* rather than *inheritors* of property. Mr. Butola felt that reducing the entire gamut of social relationship to *interpersonal* relations might not solve the problem. To him 'status' was a kind of *rhetoric*. However, Dr. A.P. Sinha took a different stand and cited examples of the Pnar families to show that interpersonal relations also mattered. He was against *oversimplification* of a *concrete* situation. Prof. Bhagawati opined that *emergent* trends could be traced rather than what was traditional and added that there was no question of coming to any kind of conclusion as to the high or low status of women. Rather one should try to examine as to how far the traditional matrilineal system provided a kind of leverage or push for enterprise/initiatives of women as was suggested by Prof. Mishra during the first Session.

When some participants said that politics was difficult for women, Dr. Baruah pointed out that one should not 'muddle' war with politics in one's attempt to cite factors. Women could easily have participated in politics. Mr. P.R. Mawthoh observes that in the Khasi-Jaintia societies non-participation of women in say, politics, had nothing to do with status connotation. Prof. Bhagawati quoted Prof. Pakem to say that it would be a mistake to consider *office holding* as an index of *political power*. Ms. Jaya Choudhury made her point that in Khasi society position of women was higher. Some would say that there was some measure of equality; while still others believed that actually the males dominated. But she cited some cases where the *Khasi males* expressed their feeling of economic *insecurity* since they do not have properties of their own under the matriliny. She was told, she said, that unlike the Khasis the Jaintia women respected their husbands as equal partners. Ms. Syiem felt that Ms Choudhury was correct to some extent. She said in her reply to Ms. Choudhury that modern changes are taking place in a transitional phase in Khasi society. The factors cited are due to change. However, traditional structure does not collapse as easily as it may be thought to do. Therefore, these problems are to be seen from long term perspectives. Dr. Gassah pointed out that one has to refer to traditional system in understanding the present situation. The *dichotomy* has to remain. The males who thought so (as Ms. Choudhury cited) might not have understood their roles in family and society.

Later, Dr. Soumen Sen intervened to observe that the deliberations on traditional Khasi-Jaintia Societies led to the emergence of two views, viz., (i) men and women enjoyed 'equal' status, and (ii) men were more dominant so far as the power structure was concerned. Raising the question as to *what was the 'actual' role of women in traditional societies*, Dr. Sen cautioned against the imposition of *our* value-judgements on our understanding of the problem. The participants agreed to a suggestion made by Mr. P. R. Mawthoh that a Seminar be organized in future for a comparative study of the status and position of women in *tribal* and *non-tribal* societies in order to facilitate better undestanding of the issues at stake.

The Seminar came to an end with a Vote of Thanks from the Chair and from the Director of the Seminar.

Mr. Henry Lamin, Lecturer, Dept. of Anthropology, NEHU.

Dr. K.M. Warjri, Lecturer, Centre for Adult & Continuing Education, NEHU.

Dr. M.P. Rina Lyngdoh, Head, Dept. of History, Shillong College, Shillong.

Dr. Biloris Lyndem, Head, Centre for Adult & Continuing Education, NEHU.

Dr. P. Nayak, Reader, Dept. of Political Science, NEHU.

Dr. K. Bhatt, Lecturer, Dept. of Anthropology, NEHU.

Dr. P.M. Passah, Lecturer, Dept. of Economics, NEHU.

Dr. L.S. Gassah, Reader, Dept. of Political Science, NEHU.

Prof. M.N. Karna, Dept. of Sociology, NEHU.

Dr. Caroline R. Marak, Dept. of English, Govt. College, Tura.

Mr. P.R. Mawthoh, Govt. of Meghalaya, Shillong.

Ms. Elizabeth Warjri, Dept. of Political Science, NEHU.

Ms. Biana Momin, Govt. College, Tura.

Mr. A. Burman, Govt. College, Tura.

Mr. M.C. Gabriel, Director of Publications, NEHU.

Dr. Apurba Baruah, Reader, Dept. of Political Science, NEHU.

Prof. A.C. Sinha, Head, Dept. of Sociology, NEHU.

Ms. Dipali Chattopadhyay, Dept. of Philosophy, Shillong College, Shillong.

Mr. Butola, Dept. of Geography, NEHU.

Dr. B. Datta Ray, Secretary, North-East India Council for Social Science Research.

Prof. A.P. Sinha, Dept. of Anthropology, NEHU.

Ms. Jaya Choudhury, Dept. of History, Shillong College, Shillong.

Dr. Soumen Sen, Head, Centre for Literary & Cultural Studies, NEHU.

Rapporteurs

Mr. Abhijit Choudhury, Dept. of History, St. Edmunds College, Shillong.

Mr. Kishore Bhattacharjee, UGC Fellow, Dept. of Anthropology, Gauhati University.

LIST OF CONTRIBUTORS

Dr. Juanita War,	Professor and Head, Department of English, North-Eastern Hill University, Kohima.
Miss I.M. Syiem,	Head, Department of Sociology, St. Edmunds College, Shillong.
Dr. L.S. Gassah,	Reader, Department of Political Science, North-Eastern Hill University, Shillong.
Dr. P.M. Passah,	Lecturer, Department of Economics, North-Eastern Hill University, Shillong.
Dr. Caroline R. Marak,	Lecturer, Department of English, Government College, Tura.
Mr.Abhijit Choudhury,	Lecturer, Department of History, St. Edmunds College, Shillong.
Dr. Soumen Sen,	Head, Centre for Literary and Cultural Studies, North-Eastern Hill University, Shillong.